WINE

For the English Edition
Editor: Susan Costello
Copy Editor: Peter Hempstead
Cover designer: Cheryl Peterka
Production manager: Louise Kurtz
Translator: Russell Stockman

First published in the United States of America in 2001 by Abbeville Press.
First published in Germany by Verlag Zabert Sandmann, Munich,
under the original title: Wein – Die praktische Schule.

First edition
10 9 8 7 6 5 4 3 2 1

Library of Congress Cataloging-in-Publication Data
Priewe, Jens.
   [Wein. English]
   Wine : a practical guide to enjoying your selection / Jens Priewe.— 1st ed.
      p. cm.
   Includes bibliographical references and index.
   ISBN 0-7892-0745-1 (alk. paper)
   1. Wine and wine making.   I. Title.
TP548.P7394613   2001
641.2'2—dc21   2001022731

WINE

A PRACTICAL GUIDE TO ENJOYING YOUR SELECTION

Jens Priewe

ABBEVILLE PRESS PUBLISHERS
New York   London

The Proper Handling of Wine

Countless people have discovered the fascination of wine in the past few years, experimenting with different wines, visiting wine-growing regions, and no longer waiting for Christmas or Easter to open a bottle. The loveliest drink in the world has become an essential element of their lives, on a par with music, theater, or literature. Increasingly, they are concerned about the proper handling of wine: how to store it, what sorts of glasses are best for it, how long it should be expected to age. More experienced wine lovers may already have discovered answers to these questions. But many of them would like to know still more. This book was written with both kinds of wine lovers in mind.

Wine—A Practical Guide shows you how to take care of wine for maximum enjoyment. How to avoid breaking a cork. Why people call a capsule a "lead" capsule even though it may be made of tin. What it means when mold has formed under a capsule. What sediment is. Which corkscrews work best. Why the formation of bubbles in the glass is a reason for complaint in a red wine but not in a white. What can happen if a Champagne is exposed too long to light, and how to hold a Champagne bottle when opening it so that it doesn't gush out.

Whenever I have eaten in a restaurant in the past few years, I have quietly watched what goes on with the waiters and sommeliers and made

Silver foil in the mouth of the bottle helps you serve wine without drips—making it a useful accessory for wine lovers.

notes. How do they quickly chill a wine? How do they warm it up if it has come up from the cellar too cool? And whenever wine collectors have invited me to visit their cellars, I have quizzed them about their experiences with vertical and horizontal storage, about raised corks, and about how they prevent the temperature in a wine cellar from fluctuating too much. When sampling wines with vineyard owners, we have compared the taste of a wine served from the bottle with that of the same wine from a carafe and learned that you should not only decant certain red wines but also certain white wines.

Such instructive conversations have helped convince me of the need for this book, as did a number of disappointing experiences—especially in restaurants: red wines served too warm, white wines ice-cold, glasses filled to the rim. Many restaurants are still somewhat unaware in their treatment of wine. Others exploit the ignorance of their guests, serving a red wine in a glass intended for white wine and refilling it so quickly that you scarcely have a chance to savor it—let alone process the alcohol. There are also plenty of wine lovers who don't have the foggiest notion about how to serve wines properly. Some go about it with antiquated ceremony, others with excessive caution.

And here's something else. Anyone who drinks fine wines needs more than one corkscrew. This book lists the various useful gadgets you will need if you decide to take wine seriously, from a capsule cutter to an aroma stopper, from a carafe holder to the computer software that will help you manage your wine cellar. Epicures may sneer at some of these accessories, but wine professionals do not find them silly at all.

That is how it is with wine. There are no simple truths. Opening a bottle, serving the wine, and tasting it—this is all simple enough if you have the perfect wine merchant coaching you every step of the way. If you don't, you need to learn on your own how to take care of the loveliest drink in the world.

The Loveliest Drink in the World

"All slightly intoxicating foodstuffs make you dream: red meat, squab, duck, game, especially hare, also asparagus, celery, truffles, vanilla . . ." —the French gastro-philosopher Jean-Anthèlme Brillat-Savarin wrote this in 1826. He forgot wine. Nearly 200 years later it is wine, especially, that makes for dreams.

Wine and the Bottle

The glass bottle is in part responsible for a wine's quality. It is thanks to the glass bottle that wine began its rise to become the noblest of all drinks. It protects the wine and preserves it. It allows a wine to age and develop. It ensures that a wine can be served and enjoyed in proper portions. Wine drinkers frequently demonstrate their respect for the bottle by keeping it even after it has been emptied.

The Front Label

This is a wine's calling card. It enhances the look of a bottle and provides important information about its contents, notably the wine's name. This can derive from its place of origin (Chablis, for example) or the grape variety from which it was made (Merlot, for example). Many wines simply carry a brand name. In addition, the label indicates the vintage, provides the name of the producer (or bottler), and locates the growing region (sometimes even the specific vineyard) from which the grapes came.

On European labels, alcohol content is stated only approximately: 12 or 12.5 percent per volume. More specific values are not permitted—in contrast to non-European wines. Moreover, the bottle's volume must be stated: 75 cl is the same as 750 ml. An "e" indicates the European standard volume measure.

The Back Label

Because of strict rules governing the front label, many producers have begun placing additional information important to the purchaser on a quasi-unofficial back label. Here they can indicate at what temperature and with what dishes the wine should be enjoyed. Often they say more about the wine's grape variety and how the wine was produced. On non-European wine labels, it is also necessary to list any added substances (sulfites, for example). Thanks to this added information, the back label is frequently more interesting than the official front one.

The Bottle

Glass is neutral in taste and therefore resistant to alcohol, tannic acid, and phenols. Green or brown glass protects the wine from the majority of infrared rays, thus preserving its color. Glass is also sturdy; if the glass is strong enough, it is possible to stack bottles up to forty high in a large cellar.

Glass survives temperatures from 5°F (−15°C) to more than 176°F (80°C)—an important factor for the transport of wine. Glass bottles can also be recycled. Because of the difficulty of cleaning them, it is more energy-saving to recycle them as crushed glass. The sole disadvantage of glass is that it is heavy and that it is easily broken.

HOW WINE CAME TO BE STORED IN BOTTLES

Glass was already known as a raw material in the early Bronze Age, but glass containers did not become common until Roman times. Wine was occasionally stored in glass even then. The first bottles specifically designed for the storage and transport of wine date from the fourteenth century, when the Venetian glass industry came into its own. At that time glass was a symbol of wealth, like gold or silver. Since glass was thin and breakable, it was protected by a sheath of woven straw. The sturdy wine bottle was invented in 1640 in Newcastle, the center of a prospering glass industry.

Glassblowers of the time boasted their new product was not only beautiful to look at but also strong enough to be used in commerce. London wine dealers required different bottle sizes and took to sealing them with an enamel seal that indicated their volume in order to avoid deception. To be sure, only good wine was destined to be "put in bottles," an expression still used by dealers today. Ordinary wines were stored either in jars of stoneware, tin, or ceramic, or in wooden casks—and were even drunk from them. Plastic containers have now replaced these humbler vessels.

The Neck of the Bottle

The neck is the bottle's most inspired feature. It confines the contact between the liquid and the air to a minimum and permits the use of a cork as a seal.

The Cork

Old-fashioned, perhaps, but still irreplaceable, cork prevents the passage of air, and thanks to its elasticity, it presses so tightly against the neck of the bottle that no liquid can escape. And cork is durable; good corks last at least twenty-five years if a cellar has adequate humidity.

The Capsule

A useful but unnecessary feature of wine packaging. It makes a bottle look nice and shows that it has not been opened. It also protects the cork from cork moths and prevents evaporation over long-term aging. Capsules are now made of tin, aluminum, or plastic. Lead capsules are no longer used.

Wine–A Delicate Substance

Wine is a highly sensitive product. Wine does not like intense light and loves cool temperatures. It also welcomes high humidity. Rooms that give people chills or feel uncomfortably damp are ideal. Such spaces are now found, if at all, only in old castles with vaulted cellars. Yet if they are constructed intelligently, modern wine cellars can approximate them.

1 Storing Temperature

The ideal temperature for storing wine is between 54°F (12°C) and 57°F (14°C). The reason for this is simply a practical one: a bottle taken from the cellar at this temperature is nearly ready to serve. In fact, wine can be properly kept at any temperature between 41°F (5°C) and 64°F (18°C). It will not suffer even at temperatures around 68°F (20°C), though alcohol evaporates faster at higher temperatures. If kept at a constant temperature of more than 77°F (25°C), a wine's aroma can change, taking on a "stewed" note (as in stewed fruit).

2 Storing Position

If wines are to be stored for many years, their bottles should lie on their sides. Corks need to maintain contact with the wine so that they do not dry out. For short-term storage, bottles can be left standing.

3 Protection from Light

A good wine cellar has no windows. Light is damaging to wine—even though nowadays most bottles are made of green or brown glass, which acts as a filter. Wines that are regularly exposed to light oxidize more rapidly. The result: Wines, especially white wines, darken, becoming a brownish color.

4 Humidity

Even though a wine is tightly sealed with a cork, there is a slight exchange of air between the inside of the bottle and the outside. Stored in a dry place, the liquid will evaporate more rapidly than it would in a well-humidified place. Eighty to 85 percent humidity is ideal. Humidity can be checked with a hygrometer.

5 Temperature Variations

An ideal temperature is a constant one. Fluctuations in temperature should be minimal. With each additional degree, a wine expands in the bottle. It will accept slight, gradual changes in temperature better than sudden leaps. Cellars that vary in temperature more than 14 degrees over the course of a year are not suited for long-term storage of wine. A thermometer is essential.

6 Shelving Systems

Wood shelving is among the most efficient possibilities in terms of space. Diagonal compartments create many small spaces and also add stability.

7 Special Sizes

Magnums, double magnums, and other odd sizes need special compartments from which they can be retrieved one at a time.

8 Sink

Before serving, a host may want to take a tiny sip from an opened bottle to test the wine's condition and check for flaws. He or she can then spit it out in the sink.

9 Cellar Manager

On a computer with special cellar software, you can easily keep track of your cellar's inventory. For the available programs, see pp. 108f.

10 Vibration

To develop properly, wines that are stored for a long time need to be undisturbed. For this reason a wine cellar should be built on a solid foundation. Vibrations from truck traffic or nearby heating units can damage a wine over an extended period.

White Wines and Red Wines

Making good wines is a craft, producing great ones is an art. Gifted cellar masters are properly considered true artists. Some are even immortalized, like the monk who invented Champagne, Dom Pérignon. They know how to give wines expressiveness and polish, and thereby ensure that the wine drinker is never bored. Even the best wine is not worthy if it is always consistently good.

White Wines

Almost all white wines are made from white grapes. They constitute slightly less than half of the wines currently produced worldwide. Most are drunk young and taste fresh and fruity. They are generally more acidic than red wines and have a somewhat lower alcohol content.

A few first-class white wines (non-European Chardonnays, for example, or white wines from Burgundy) nevertheless strive more for ripeness and fullness than freshness and acid. But some of these can have an alcohol content of more than 14 percent per volume. The best can survive for 25 years or more. Yet good, acid-toned white wines (great Rieslings from Germany, Alsace, and the Wachau, for example) can also look forward to long-term aging.

Rosé Wines

Rosés are made from red grapes. The must and the skins (containing pigment) are separated after only a few hours, which prevents most of the pigment from passing into the must. As a result the wine has a light red tint instead of a deep color. In terms of type, rosés are white wines. Industrially produced rosé wines and some rosé Champagnes consist of a mix of white and red wines.

Red wine is produced from red grapes. It is distinguished by its higher tannin content.

White wine is generally drunk young, but there are white wines that are capable of aging.

Semi-Sparkling Wines

These are wines with a little car-bonation, usually added artificially—as in mineral water. In France, these Champagne-like wines are labeled either *pétillant* (stronger) or *perlant* (weaker), in Italy *frizzante*. In Germany, they are re-ferred to as *Perlweine*. The bottles are stopped with a simple cork, without a wire cage. Simple Proseccos are typical semi-sparkling wines.

Semi-sparkling wines contain a small amount of carbon dioxide, most of it added artificially.

sé wines, with only a few eptions, are white wines de from red grapes.

ENJOYING WINES

How and when wines should be drunk has occupied people since wines were first developed. When a reporter asked Baron Elie de Roth-schild how he preferred to drink his precious red Lafite and on what occasions, the baron snapped, "Stop jabbering," and refused further com-ment. However Lily Bollinger, patron-ess of the Champagne house of the same name, responded to a similar question, "I drink Champagne when I'm happy and I drink it when I'm sad. I enjoy it when I'm alone and when I'm in a crowd. If I don't have any appetite, I open a bottle, and if I'm hungry I do the same. Otherwise, I don't touch it—unless I'm thirsty."

Red Wines

Red wines are always made from red grapes. Most are heavier than white wines, especially those produced in southern growing regions. But there are also light-red wines, such as Beaujolais, Kalterer See, or Germany's Dornfelder.

What distinguishes red wines is their tannins. These are extracted from the grape peels during fermentation. In addi-tion to their fruity primary aroma, wines rich in tannins (Bordeaux, Brunellos di Montalcino, Barolos, Riojas) frequently present secondary aromas of spices (cloves, cinnamon, black pepper), balsam (pine, vanilla, leather), or vegetables (eucalyptus, mint, tobacco). A great deal of tannin means that the wines must ripen in wood, and can later improve over a long period in the bottle.

Special Wines

Special wines generally come from specific growing regions. They are produced by special processes and are consumed on special occasions. Nearly all of them were discovered by accident, and it was only later that specialists came to understand the conditions that led to the coincidence.

Champagnes

The creation of Champagne became possible only after the invention of a thick-walled bottle that could withstand the pressure of the carbon dioxide. The French insist that the bubbles enhance the wine's bouquet and refine its taste. Other countries have their own fizzy wines: Spain its Cava, Italy its Franciacorta (and other Spumantis), Germany and Austria their Sekte.

France also has many *crémants*— sparkling wines with a touch of carbon dioxide—in addition to Champagne. The pressure of a crémant is roughly 3 atmospheres, while that of a Champagne ranges between 5 and 6 atmospheres. That is three times the pressure of an automobile tire. For economic reasons, ordinary sparkling wines and Sekt are now fermented in stainless steel tanks rather than in the bottle.

"Liqueur wine" is the catch-all term for wines containing at least 15 percent alcohol.

Botrytized Wines

These wines with a concentrated sweetness are mostly made from white grapes and are some of the most expensive wines in the world. They have nothing to do with ordinary sweet wines. They are produced wholly or in part from withered grapes infected with botrytis, or "noble rot," and containing little juice. The most famous botrytized wines are the Hungarian Tokays, German and Austrian Beerenausleses and Trockenbeerenausleses, Alsatian Grains Nobles, Sauternes from Bordeaux, Monbazillac from Bergerac, and Quart-de-Chaumes from the Loire.

Port is a noble Portuguese red wine that is fortified with brandy.

The wines themselves contain no fungus spores and have no taste of rot.

Sherry

The Andalusians drink Sherry with shrimp. Outside of Spain, Sherry is considered a classic aperitif wine. It is made from white grapes. The dry variant is called "Fino" or "Manzanilla," which has a spicy, salty aroma. Sherry is laced with brandy. A good Sherry therefore contains roughly 16 percent alcohol. Sweet Sherrys, called "olorosos," can have as much as 18 percent. They are dark in color and have a spicy, caramel-like taste.

Liqueur Wines

The catch-all term for wines with at least 15 percent alcohol. Included, in addition to the fortified wines (Port, Sherry, Madeira, Banyuls, Marsala), are mainly wines of concentrated sweetness from warm growing regions that are made from overripe grapes or grapes dried on straw. The most famous liqueur wine is Tuscany's vin santo. But liqueur wines are also produced in France, Spain, and outside Europe—some of them with the addition of sweet-grape must.

Port

Port is a sweet Portuguese red wine that is fortified with a small amount of brandy. It contains roughly 18 to 20 percent alcohol. It is a heavy, fiery, fruity wine that can be extremely elegant if it is of high quality. Vintage Ports can easily age in bottles for a hundred years. Its color ranges from dark red in youth to mahogany brown in old age.

Sherry is a classic aperitif wine fortified with brandy.

Sparkling wines are those that are naturally carbonated: Sekt, Cava, Champagne, also some Proseccos.

Opening the Wine Bottle

Opening a wine bottle is more than a mechanical process. It is the last act before the grand finale, before the moment when the wine, after a stormy fermentation and frequently long years of aging in the barrel, surrenders its secret at last.

Removing the Capsule

Capsules are there for looks. They help decorate the bottle. Most capsules are made of plastic or tinfoil. Properly removing them is not always easy—but there is no special trick to it if you have the right tools.

The capsule cutter was the invention of a Texas millionaire. Wine lovers all over the world are grateful.

The Capsule Cutter

With this device, any capsule can be r moved quickly and easily. Simply pla the capsule cutter against the top of t bottle and turn. Rolling blades cut throu the capsule cleanly, no matter what is made of. Then you simply lift off t top of the capsule. A capsule cutter al works with magnum bottles and cos only a few dollars. Its only disadvantag You always have to have one han Some corkscrews have a built-in capsu cutter. If they don't, you have to use knife. But how do you do it? And esp cially where do you cut? It is immateri as far as the capsule is concerned, but does matter to the wine.

Plastic Capsule with Tab: Lift up the tab with a fingernail, then pull it all the way around the capsule. The top of the capsule simply falls off.

Tinfoil Capsule with Perforation: Bend back the tab with a fingernail and carefully pull it all the way around. Lift off the top of the capsule.

Cutting with a Knife: Place the blade against the capsule at the top of the flare of the bottle and press gently while twisting the bottle. The capsule then lifts off easily.

Awkward: If you place the knife against the bottom edge of the flare it is still difficult to remove the top of the capsule.

Dangerous: If you place the knife against the lip of the bottle, the wine flows across the cut as you pour and particles of metal can find their way into the glass.

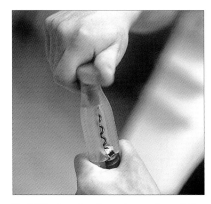

Unsightly: Inserting the corkscrew through the capsule and tearing it open with the rising cork, then peeling away what is left.

CAPSULE RECYCLING

Tinfoil capsules are environmentally friendly, for they can be almost 100 percent recycled. It is worthwhile to remove all the foil from empty wine bottles and save it. Even melting down the bottle glass with fragments of the capsule still attached is not harmful to the environment, because no poisonous gases are produced— in contrast to the burning of PVC or polyester. Since tin pulverizes at 392°F (200°C), it can be easily separated out when melting the glass and reused after cooling.

The Function of the Capsule

A capsule is meant to guarantee that a wine has not been tampered with—an increasingly important function in an age of wine forgeries. Moreover, it slows the exchange of gases between the inside and the outside of the bottle. Finally, a capsule can protect the wine from a dangerous pest—the cork moth.

Capsule Materials

Expensive wines almost always come with a capsule made of tin. Tin has taken the place of lead, the traditional material; lead capules are now found only on wines from old vintages. Tin is also a heavy metal, but unlike lead, it is non-toxic. Tin is soft, malleable, and clings so tightly to the neck of the bottle that it almost completely prevents air from coming into contact with the wine. Tin capsules have only one disadvantage: they are expensive. Aluminum capsules are cheaper and also protect the cork very well, but aluminum is a light metal. It does have the elegance of tin, and it is possible to cut yourself on the sharp edges when you open the bottle.

Originating in California only recently but already widespread there is the practice of omitting the capsule altogether and sealing the bottle instead with a button of beeswax between the top of the cork and the lip of the bottle.

The Influence on the Wine

Since 1960, researchers have attempted to discover whether metal capsules can have a detrimental effect on wines. All studies have shown that within an aging period of ten years virtually no particles from a lead capsule transfer to the wine.

After ten years, however, the wine can have a higher lead content than it had when first bottled: if, for example, the cork is too short and completely saturated, and the thin layer of tin with which even lead capsules are plated has been destroyed. The possibility of damage to the wine is even less with modern tin capsules. Acids and alcohol do not corrode tin, and inorganic tin compounds are not poisonous. Moreover, wines intended for long aging are now provided with longer corks than they used to be.

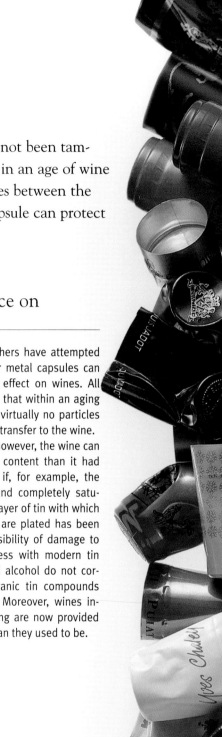

Bottle capsules: Most are made of plastic, the best ones of tinfoil.

Unperforated Capsule: When properly affixed, it seals the bottle almost completely, thus limiting evaporation. It also protects against cork moths.

Sludge: When wine comes into contact with the woody lenticels of the cork, a slimy substance is formed. It does not damage the wine but must be removed.

Perforated Capsule: Has the advantage of allowing moisture to evaporate so that no sludge forms. One disadvantage is that the cork moth can lay its eggs underneath the capsule.

Mildew: In damp cellars, mildew can form under perforated capsules. It does no damage to either the cork or the taste of the wine.

THE CORK MOTH

The cork moth (Nemapogon coacellus) is a tiny insect no more than one-quarter of an inch (7 mm) long. It loves dark, damp rooms and is commonly found in wine cellars. It lays its eggs on the top of a cork. The newly hatched larvae eat into the cork, and as a result, it becomes porous, gets saturated, and develops mold. Today's generally higher temperatures in wine cellars have only encouraged the pest. The same is true of the cellar moth (Dryadaula pactolia) and wine moth (Oenophilia v-flavum). The latter prefers dry cellars. The best protection against moths is an unperforated capsule.

Removing the Cork

Pulling a cork from the neck of a bottle elegantly and cleanly can be a test of strength—especially if you lack the proper tool. With modern corkscrews, provided you use them properly, opening a bottle of wine can be a breeze.

Grip and Spindle

The use of a corkscrew is not instinctive. It has to be learned. And learning in this case does not begin with muscle training but rather shopping around for the right type of corkscrew. For decades the gadget was unimproved, consisting of only a grip and a helical spindle. You twisted the spindle into the cork, then pulled on the grip. A seemingly simple operation.

Yet millions of corks were probably pressed into the bottle while inserting the spindle, and countless numbers of others destroyed by the use of excessive force when pulling, for corks can be lodged in the neck of the bottle quite firmly. When inserted, corks are compressed to roughly two-thirds of their diameter. The pressure they exert against the glass is greater than that in an automobile tire. Moreover, most corks are given a coating of wax. Under normal conditions the wax makes it easier to remove the cork, but if the wine has been exposed to excessive heat, the wax can also act like a glue.

It's All in How You Pull

Today there is an array of corkscrews from which to choose. None of them is perfect. All of them, to be sure, comprise more than a simple grip and spindle. In any case, a good corkscrew should be easy to use.

The cork should slide slowly and surely out of the neck of the bottle without having to pull. Slowly, because a loud "pop" can damage the wine. Good wines are stressed by the sudden equalization of pressure and inrush of oxygen into the bottle.

In the model pictured to the left, a Screwpull, this danger is avoided. The bottle can even stand on the table while the cork is withdrawn. One hand presses the two arms against the neck of the bottle, the other twists the handle.

A good corkscrew is one that is easy to use. The cork slides out of the bottle slowly, gently, and safely.

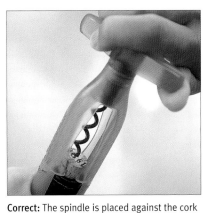

Correct: The spindle is placed against the cork vertically and inserted into the center of the cork's surface.

Incorrect: The spindle is not inserted vertically and bores into the cork at an angle. The cork crumbles once you begin to pull.

Correct: The spindle must pass completely through the cork to withdraw it easily. You can tell from the decreased resistance when the tip of the spindle emerges from bottom.

Incorrect: The spindle is too short to pass through the long cork. Tightly seated corks are difficult to withdraw and are likely to crumble.

Correct: To open a bottle with a T-shaped corkscrew, hold it in front of you and slowly ease the cork from the neck of the bottle by gently flexing your upper arm.

Incorrect: Pulling the cork from the bottle with all your strength can stress the wine, owing to the sudden change from a vacuum to normal pressure once the cork leaves the bottle.

THE SPINDLE

The most important part of the corkscrew is the spindle. First, it must be long enough to be able to completely pass through even the longest corks commonly in use (about 2.5 inches [60 mm]). Second, it must not be too thick, so that the cork cells suffer minimal damage when it is inserted. High-priced corkscrews are also elastic and coated with Teflon, so that they slide through the cork easily. It is also important that the spindle has

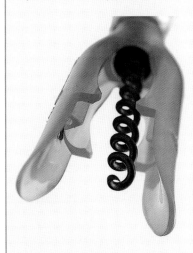

enough twists. The more there are, the easier it is to withdraw the cork. Finally, the diameter of the twists must be large enough to allow a wooden match to pass through the center. If it is, there is little danger of breaking the cork as you pull.

Broken Cork—Now What?

Corks frequently break when you open a bottle. Generally, it is because you inserted the corkscrew at an angle or failed to twist it through the full length of the cork. But sometimes corks simply crumble because they are old and dry. For professionals with special tools, this is no problem, but for ordinary wine lovers it can be catastrophic.

No Catastrophe

For some wine lovers, the crumbling of a cork can be a major crisis. They try wedging the remaining portion of the cork out of the neck of the bottle with a knitting needle or the point of a pair of scissors, and in the process generally destroy it so completely that the surface of the wine is covered with a thick layer of cork dust leaving them wondering whether they can still enjoy the wine at all. But it does not necessarily have to be a disaster. There are several ways to carefully remove a broken cork from a bottle. The first rule is not to damage it further, and if possible to get it out in one piece. The corkscrew is not always the ideal tool for this. If the cork is saturated, old, or crumbling, a butler's friend is recommended. If you do not have one handy, there are other methods of clearing the neck of the bottle, but they require a certain skill and a lot of patience.

If you are clumsy and crumble what is left of the cork, you should at least know how to get the cork dust out of the bottle. Pour out a small quantity of the wine into either a sink or a separate glass. Cork fragments floating on the surface will generally flow out with the first few drops, leaving the rest of the wine free of them.

Corks in which the lenticels run horizontally break more easily.

Second Try: If the cork has broken off in the upper part of the neck and is still tight, it is possible to use a corkscrew again.

Risky: If the cork has broken in the lower part of the neck, there is the danger that it will fall into the bottle if you try to spear it with the corkscrew.

Surefire: A butler's friend is a safe way of removing broken corks. Insert the blades carefully between the cork and the glass . . .

Slick: . . . then remove the cork from the neck of the bottle with gentle twisting movements. You may have to grasp it a second time.

Last Resort: You can press the lodged fragment of the cork into the bottle with the handle of a teaspoon, but if the bottle is very full, the wine may spurt out.

Decant: If a fragment of cork is floating on the top of the wine, you will have to decant it into a carafe. Use the teaspoon handle to keep the cork from blocking the flow.

A "MIDWIFE" MAY HELP

There is a tool, called a "midwife," specifically designed to fish fragments of cork out of a bottle. It is available only in special shops. Sliding the collar up and down causes the arms to open and close. If you are skillful and patient, you can grasp any cork particles floating on the wine and lift them out through the neck. But the midwife is no good if the cork has broken in half, for it cannot pull it out. It is also no help with tiny crumbs or cork dust.

The Classic Corkscrews

Without a corkscrew you would have to break a wine bottle to get at its contents. But the selection of corkscrews is large, greater than one person could need. Most are complex and unwieldy, and require strength. Only a few are really recommended—those that do not pull the cork so much as lift or lever it out from the neck of the bottle.

Waiter's Friend

The simplest, safest, and most common corkscrew. You flip out the spindle, twist it into the cork until the brace comes into contact with the lip of the bottle. Then you simply pry out the cork. A certain amount of strength and skill are required. It comes with a built-in capsule knife. *Disadvantage:* The spindle is frequently too short, and with long corks you may have to repeat the process.

- ＋ ＋ compact
- ＋ ＋ breakproof
- ＋ easy to use
- － saves effort
- ＋ ＋ inexpensive

Pulltap

A refinement of the waiter's friend invented by French sommeliers. It differs from the waiter's friend in that the brace is in two sections with notches at different heights, allowing you to remove a long cork with a single insertion of the spindle. *Advantage:* The pulltap also has a built-in capsule knife.

- ＋ ＋ compact
- ＋ ＋ breakproof
- ＋ easy to use
- ＋ saves effort
- ＋ ＋ inexpensive

Screwpull Elite

One of the best and most ingenious corkscrews in the world. It comes from France. Simply set it on the top of the bottle, then twist the spindle into the cork and keep twisting until the cork safely rises out of the bottle by itself. *Advantages:* Long, elastic, Teflon-coated spindle; wide-diameter helix; and a built-in capsule knife. *Disadvantage:* You cannot use it if the bottle has a wide lip.

- ＋ compact
- ＋ breakproof
- ＋ ＋ easy to use
- ＋ ＋ saves effort
- ＋ inexpensive

T Corkscrew

The simplest of all corkscrews is available in numerous versions: with handles made of wood, sterling silver, or horn, or Day-Glo plastic. Though indestructible, it is impractical, as it requires too much strength.

+ compact
+ + breakproof
− easy to use
− − saves effort
+ + inexpensive

Butterfly

A cumbersome but very popular postwar model, it was once in every household. Many people still rely on the device, since it removes corks safely and with relatively little effort. Place the foot on the top of the bottle with the point of the spindle in the center of the cork. Twisting in the spindle can be awkward, since the bottle needs to stand on the table and is therefore much too high. *Advantage:* A gentle removal of the cork is guaranteed.

− compact
+ breakproof
+ easy to use
+ + saves effort
+ inexpensive

Bottlepull

A corkscrew developed in Austria that is simple in function, easy to use, and inexpensive. The thin stainless steel spindle with its relatively wide diameter is capable of pulling even the tightest corks. *Advantages:* Built-in capsule knife with a serrated blade that is especially good for cutting plastic capsules. The handle can be removed for compact storage. A good corkscrew for travelers.

+ + compact
+ breakproof
+ + easy to use
+ + saves effort
+ + inexpensive

High-Tech Corkscrews

The simplest corkscrews are by no means always the best. They strain your biceps and stress the wine with a loud pop when the bottle finally releases the cork. On the other hand, many corkscrews or cork lifters that remove the cork gently and quietly are monstrous-looking gadgets that take up too much room in a kitchen drawer.

Butler's Friend

A cork puller developed in America that is especially effective with old, crumbling, and thoroughly saturated corks. The two blades are inserted to their full length between the glass and the cork. Because they are of different lengths, the cork is firmly grasped during extraction and can be gently removed, if necessary with a gentle twist. *Disadvantage:* Inserting the blades requires a certain amount of skill.

  + + compact
  + + breakproof
     – easy to use
     – saves effort
  + + inexpensive

Cork Pops 2

A compressed gas cork remover that requires expensive cartridges. You insert the stainless steel needle vertically through the cork, making certain that it sticks out the bottom. Pressing the thumb on the cartridge releases gas into the bottle and the increased pressure lifts the cork. The gadget functions safely, swiftly, and effortlessly. *Disadvantages:* It is difficult to remove the cork from the syringe, and if you're not careful you can stab yourself.

     – compact
     + breakproof
     – easy to use
  + + saves effort
  – – inexpensive

Winemaster VacuVin

This high-tech corkscrew from the Vacu-Vin firm is huge, but engineered down to the last detail. The device is firmly mounted on the bottle. Pressing down the small levers gently slides the spindle into the cork; the large levers lift it out. Returning the levers to their original position frees the cork from the spindle. *Disadvantages:* Long corks can be a problem, and after roughly 800 uses the spindle has to be replaced.

  – – compact
  + + breakproof
  + + easy to use
  + + saves effort
  – – inexpensive

Puigpull

A corkscrew from Spain that represents a further development of the waiter's friend. With the help of a notched track the cork is withdrawn from the bottle in a series of levered lifts rather than a single pull. The amount of strength required is therefore minimal. Built-in capsule knife. *Disadvantages:* Using the device requires a little practice; also, the spindle is too short.

+ + compact
  − breakproof
− − easy to use
+ + saves effort
+ + inexpensive

Prosecco Corkscrew

This model was originally developed for sparkling wines, but it works just as well for any wine. Placing it on the cork is somewhat complicated, and the bottle must stand firm. Because of its size, twisting the spindle into the cork can be a clumsy balancing act. But removing the cork by squeezing the pistol grip is virtually effortless.

− − compact
  + breakproof
− − easy to use
+ + saves effort
  − inexpensive

Leverpull

A high-tech model. The pliers grip the neck of the bottle, and the spindle is easily inserted into the cork by pressing a lever (not twisting). When you release the lever, the cork slides swiftly and safely out of the bottle. *Disadvantages:* The spindle is easily broken if you are in a hurry (replacements are included), and there is no built-in capsule knife.

− − compact
  + breakproof
+ + easy to use
+ + saves effort
− − inexpensive

Opening Champagne Bottles

Champagne is usually served on festive occasions—pity that the exertions of even experienced wine lovers still make for wet hands. But relax: even professionals can let the cork exit from the bottle with too much noise and have the precious wine bubble out.

If the Champagne bubbles out, it is because the bottle was either subjected to too much motion or set down too hard.

When Corks Pop . . .

. . . and the bubbly spews out, there's often a sense of panic instead of conviviality. A soaked tablecloth and startled guests are the least of it; worse is the stained clothing, as well as a bottle that is now only half full. The most common reasons are that the bottle was jostled too much before being opened or set down on the table too roughly. With sparkling wines that have previously lain in a horizontal position, a jolt such as this can create enormous pressure inside the bottle. With gentle handling and careful opening, nothing should happen. There is still the problem of how to prevent the wine from bubbling up out of the glass when serving. The answer is simple: pour only half as much, then add more after the mousse, or foam, has settled.

Step 1: Most sparkling wines have a tear-off strip. Grasp the end of it and pull open the capsule along the perforation.

Step 2: Feel under the tinfoil for the lift-up wire. Raise it with the fingers and tear back the rest of the capsule.

Step 3: Twist the wire to open the cage; loosen the wires ringing the neck of the bottle and carefully lift away the cage.

Step 4: Grip the cork firmly in one hand (using a hand towel if one is handy), and carefully twist the bottle with the other (not vice versa).

Step 5: Once the cork is loosened, it is immediately under pressure. Carefully exert counterpressure with the thumb, so that it does not shoot out.

Step 6: Corks that will not budge can be loosened with Champagne pliers. But this only loosens the cork; it will still be necessary to twisting it out by hand.

HOW TO PREVENT THE WINE FROM SPEWING OUT

If you set a bottle of sparkling wine down too hard, the cork is bound to shoot up. You should never open the bottle in a vertical position. Keep it at an angle even while removing the capsule and the cage. The cork too should be extracted while holding it at an angle. The wine is thus exposed to the maximum amount of air inside the bottle. The foam that builds up as a result of the equalizing pressure settles quickly. Beer lovers are familiar with the same problem. When pouring, be sure to hold the glass at angle in order to avoid excess buildup of foam.

Cork and Its Substitutes

Cork as a wine bottle stopper is being debated. Some wines present an unpleasant corky taste or musty note. Many wine lovers cannot understand why vintners continue to use a material that can spoil their wines and requires complicated tools

Natural Corks

Most wine bottles are sealed with natural cork. Since it is stamped in one piece out of the bark of the cork oak (Quercus suber), it is also the most expensive type of seal. In general, it meets all the requirements of a high-quality bottle stopper. It presses tightly against the neck of the bottle, is highly durable, is neutral in taste, and is a natural product—like the wine itself. Taste faults can usually be traced to its processing and aging. More than half the cork used comes from Portugal. Smaller cork producers are Sardinia, North Africa, Spain, and France. The trees are cultivated on plantations, so cork production is no threat to nature, though the raw material has now become scarce, owing to increased wine production.

Laminated Corks

In this variant of pressed cork a slice of whole cork is glued to the bottom. The laminate reduces the frequency of taste faults, but only in wines consumed within a year. Faults can occur if the wine comes into contact with the pressed cork.

Pressed Cork

The cheapest cork variant is made up of fragments of cork that are granulated and glued together. Pressed corks are most frequently associated with musty or corky tones, and their production has nearly doubled in the last ten years.

to remove, especially since there are bottle stoppers that are easier to use and safer. Cork has become replaceable in terms of technology, but not in terms of psychology. To a majority of wine lovers, corks are sacred.

Plastic Corks

Stoppers made of polyethylene have found widespread use in recent years. Many ordinary wines, especially in America but also in Italy and in Spain, now come with these colorful cork substitutes. They are leakproof, they do not produce musty notes, and they can be easily removed with an ordinary corkscrew. Needless to say, they differ in quality. The best silicone stoppers come from America and are produced by the extrusion process. They have proven successful especially for white wines. For red wines, which are aged longer, it is not yet certain whether the plastic is affected by phenols and tannic acid or whether the polyethylene hastens the decomposition of sulfuric acids, allowing the wine to oxidize more rapidly.

Screw Caps

Screw caps are widely used in the liquor industry and have become relatively common even for wines. They seal the bottle nearly airtight and leave no trace in the wine's taste. Moreover, they are easy to use. But the majority of wine drinkers will accept them only on jug wines.

Crown Corks

The crown cork is the cheapest bottle stopper. It seals the bottle nearly airtight. And the plastic insert has no effect on the quality of the wine. Although bottles of the finest Champagnes wear only a crown cork during their three-year aging, this stopper has not proved popular for either ordinary wines or better-quality vintages.

What Makes a Good Cork?

The cork's most important task is to provide a secure seal—secure in the sense that there is no leakage and as little air gets into the bottle as possible. Wines that are consumed quickly are sealed with short corks, whereas wines that require aging need longer corks.

A look at a cork's interior reveals large, woody lenticels lurking behind its pores.

Cork—A Natural Substance

Cork is composed of the dead cells of the bark of the cork oak. The cells contain nitrogen, and their walls are composed of suberin, a waterproof substance. This is what prevents liquid from escaping through the cork in a bottle. It is also difficult for air to penetrate the cell walls, and for this reason, a bottle sealed with cork makes for ideal aging. Cork is also elastic. In the neck of the bottle, it is compressed to almost half its natural size. It presses tight against the glass, ensuring that no liquid can seep past it.

Its dark veins and pores are called lenticels. In nature, they furnish the tree with oxygen through the dead bark, but they can be a headache for the wine drinker. Wine and oxygen can pass through them into the interior of the cork. The more lenticels there are, the poorer the cork's quality. The poorer the quality the faster the oxidation of the wine—and the greater the danger of taste faults. Bottle corks are bleached with hydrogen peroxide to sterilize them and make them look nicer. They are also waxed. Without wax it is extremely difficult to press them into the neck of the bottle, and even more difficult to remove them.

No two corks are alike. One may permit a greater exchange of air, another less. Thus a wine from one bottle may be fresher than the same wine from a different bottle. Even a layperson can tell whether a cork is of high or only mediocre quality simply by looking at it.

High Quality: With a high-quality cork, almost completely free of lenticels, there is almost no exchange of air. Corky tastes are infrequent.

Standard: Since a standard cork has only a moderate number of lenticels, it is difficult for wine to penetrate it.

Low Quality: A cork laced with vertical lenticels becomes saturated easily. It may crumble, thus endangering the taste of the wine.

High Elasticity: Cork is an extremely elastic material, for it consists of up to 95 percent gas. Before bottling, a typical cork has a diameter of about 1 inch (25 mm) (the part outside the bottle). In the neck of the bottle it is compressed to about half an inch (15.5 mm).

SATURATED CORKS

After fifteen or twenty years of aging, many corks are completely saturated with wine. As long as the bottles do not leak and the interior of the cork is not infected with bacteria, this is no cause for concern; saturated corks cannot dry out. After twenty years, however, even the best corks gradually soften. If the wine is still not consumed and is meant to age still longer, it is advisable to have the bottle recorked. The large Bordeaux Châteaux provide this service routinely at no cost, though collectors have to take their bottles to Bordeaux. At that time any space in the bottle that has resulted from evaporation of the wine is replaced with young wine. Quality-conscious vintners in other regions routinely recork customers' bottles as well.

Corky Wines

It is estimated that from 5 to 8 percent of all corks are flawed, and the percentage is rising. The cork devil can strike young and old wines, whites and reds alike. Even Champagnes can have a corky taste. Consumers are powerless. In a restaurant, patrons can send the wine back, but wine dealers and vintners do not provide replacements for the restaurant owners.

Unpalatable

No one can tell whether a wine is corky before the bottle has been opened. Neither mold nor saturation is a sure indication that the cork is infected. Smell is the first sign, for a corked wine smells musty. Sometimes the corky note becomes apparent only in the taste, which is often overpowered by the cork. Cork-sick wines are almost always unpalatable.

Trichloranisol

An infected cork can seem okay on the outside. The chief cause of the bad taste is a chlorine compound that does not affect the cork's appearance. It is called "2, 4, 6 trichloranisol," abbreviated TCA, and is perceptible even in the tiniest quantities: as little as 10 ppt (parts per thousand) suffices to completely spoil the taste of a wine. TCA is the metabolic product of a group of molds that feed on chlorine compounds. These molds do not inhabit the outside of the cork, however, and are not even visible. The coincidence of chlorine and the molds is therefore

A microwave-heated Delfin cork.

a great danger to the cork. If it occurs, it will happen in the interior of the cork, or more precisely in the lenticels, where the molds like to live. The more open pores, or lenticel entrances, a cork exhibits, the greater the possibility that mold spores and chlorine may penetrate the cork. Molds are among the normal flora of cork

oak forests, and it is no surprise that they continue to colonize the cork bark after it has been peeled from the trunk. Mold can also attack the cork during storage. But cork bark is disinfected before processing, and all mold cultures ought to be destroyed in the process.

Universal Chlorine

Chlorine is introduced during cork processing. It used to be that chlorine was used to bleach it—a free meal for molds. Today the usual bleaching agent is hydrogen peroxide. But chlorine is still widely used. In many southern European countries, tap water is chlorinated—and cork bark has to be washed before it can be processed. Chlorine is also used in many cleaning agents used to scrub wine-cellar floors, the beds of trucks used to transport cork, and the pallets on which cork is delivered. Also, any number of cleaning agents used in the home contain chlorine, though wine drinkers may not realize it. Corks that have not been fully disinfected can thus build up TCA either in the hands of the shipper or the wine dealer or in the consumer's own home.

A Bestalon cork that is washed in suberase.

Searching for Causes

TCA is the most common substance—but not the only one—that produces faults in wines. Germs and mold spores of all possible types can nest in the lenticels. Especially in spaces that are warm and damp, microorganisms can multiply and develop unpleasant flaws in a wine. Wine growers blame cork factories for failing to take the necessary precautions in the storage, sorting, and disinfection of the bark. Cork factories blame cork dealers and the vineyards for not maintaining proper hygiene in their storerooms and cellars. In truth, traditional disinfection methods are not strong enough to prevent every fault that can occur in a wine.

New Impregnation Procedure

To save the cork as a bottle seal, new procedures have been developed in recent years to attack faults in wine. One of these is impregnation with Bestalon. Corks are first washed for roughly an hour in a special water bath containing, in addition to ethanol, a small quantity of phenolic oxidase, an enzyme preparation on a suberase base developed in Denmark. It renders harmless the tannic-tasting phenoles in the cork. To be specific: they are polymerized and thus neutralized in taste. (At the same time, unpleasant-smelling anisoles are extracted.) Since the suberase enzyme also makes the surface of the cork waterproof and impregnates it, the possibility of liquid penetrating the cork is considerably lessened.

Delfin Procedure

Even higher expectations are pinned on the Delfin procedure (Direct Environmental Load Focussed Inactivation) developed in Germany. In it, all corks are run through a special chamber in which they are heated by means of electromagnetic waves. Unlike traditional sterilization with hot water, the microwaves pass completely through the cork, destroying all chemical and microbacterial impurities. Delfin corks have been on the market since 2000. Wine drinkers can only find out from the vintner whether a given wine was sealed with a Delfin or Bestalon cork.

Corkiness can generally be detected simply by smell.

How Does Wine Breathe in the Bottle?

The rate at which a red wine matures depends on its grape variety, its region of origin, its vintage, and in no small measure on the quality of the cork. A long-lived wine is provided with a cork at least 1.5 inches (40 mm) long to limit the amount of oxygen passing into the bottle. This allows the wine to breathe more slowly and age better.

Breathing and Evaporation

The small space of air between the surface of the wine and the cork (known as "ullage") is sufficient to provide the wine with oxygen for a few years and allow it to "breathe." That means that even if no air passes through the cork the wine can improve in the bottle for a few years. There are no wines with airtight seals. Even the highest-quality cork cannot completely cut off the exchange of air with the outside. Oxygen enters the bottle, and alcohol and water evaporate. Anyone can see that the level of an old wine is lower than that of a young one, which indicates that liquid has evaporated. In such cases, a wine drinker should consider consuming the wine soon, for the lower the level the more oxygen in the bottle, and the greater the wine's contact with oxygen, the faster it oxidizes. As the level sinks, the aging process speeds up exponentially. The surface contact between wine and the oxygen is especially large if the bottle is stored horizontally (1968 Gran Reserva 904, La Rioja Alta). The smallest surface is presented in a wine aged vertically (1959 Rioja Gran Reserva Ygay). The only risk to vertical aging is that the cork can dry out.

The longer the wine ages the greater the contact with air inside the bottle.

HOW AIR EXCHANGE TAKES PLACE

The exchange of gases between the inside and the outside of a bottle takes place between the cork and the neck of a bottle. Under a microscope, it can be seen that the inner wall of a bottle neck is rough and uneven. Even an elastic cork cannot press tightly enough to completely prevent the passage of air. Water and alcohol evaporate through the tiny cracks and holes, and oxygen from the outside forces its way in. Corks with many pores and imperfections only encourage the exchange of gases, so that the wine ages more rapidly. If the cork dries out and shrinks, and more and more of the bottle's contents evaporates, it is no longer a matter of the wine "breathing"— it simply oxidizes.

CORK UNDER AN ELECTRON MICROSCOPE

A normal cork consists of billions of cells filled with nitrogen. They are packed tightly together with no spaces between them. The cell walls are made of cellulose and a substance called suberin. Suberin repels water. Alcohol, oil, and air also have difficulty penetrating suberin. For this reason, only a very small amount of oxygen manages to find its way into the bottle through the cork tissue itself.

High Fill Level: This Château Latour 1990 has only $\frac{1}{2}$ inch (1 cm) of air between the surface of the wine and the bottom of the cork.

Low Level as a Result of Evaporation: This Château Latour 1982 already shows about an inch (2 cm) of air between the surface of the wine and the bottom of the cork.

Low Level as a Result of Cork Shrinkage: In this Château Latour 1968 the space between the surface of the wine and the bottom of the cork has already widened to 1.5 inches (4 cm).

Serving Wine

When wine first flows from a bottle, there is a release of tension. The wine is leaving its prison. But serving is not only an act of liberation. It is a process that requires finesse.

How to Serve Wine

Opening a bottle of wine is an exciting
moment, and experienced hosts allow their
guests to share in it, opening the bottle
at the table where all can watch. It is a
practice with a long tradition and is
meant to demonstrate that a special
wine is being served rather than an
inexpensive blend—a ruse that
was once common enough even
in high society.

A decanter basket is not
merely decoration. It was
invented to hold older
red wines that contain
sediment.

Serving with Style

Wine should be poured carefully, not simply splashed into a glass. If it is a fine
wine, the host may even pick up the
glass, tilt it at an angle with the neck of
the bottle, and let the wine slowly flow
into it. Normally, however, the glass is left
on the table while the wine is poured. If
bubbles form in the glass, there is no
need for concern, for this allows the wine
to aerate immediately, and in a minute or
so the bubbles disappear. To prevent any
wine from dripping onto the tablecloth,
practiced servers twist the bottle with
their forearm after pouring so that the
last drops cling to the lip of the bottle. If
the wine is lying in a decanter basket, do
not remove it when refilling the glasses;
instead, pick up both basket and bottle,
and pour again.

Testing the Cork: Before serving a wine you should smell the cork. Bad corks can be identified by their smell.

Cleaning: Before serving, wipe the lip of the bottle with a napkin. Using the damp end of the cork for this purpose is frowned upon.

Testing the Wine: After opening the bottle, pour a small amount in your own glass first and test the wine—with only a tiny sip.

Pouring the Wine: If you find the wine adequate, you may proceed to serve your guests, filling your own glass last.

Presenting the Cork: When fine wines are served, the cork is placed on the table in a silver plate.

Pretentious: In restaurants, the cork is often secured to the neck of the bottle with the tinfoil strip from the capsule. At home this is unnecessary—and downright pretentious.

TIPS & TRICKS: REMOVING WINE STAINS

It is often said that the most expensive part of an occasion at which wine is served is paying for the laundering of stained clothing and table linen. Spots of red wine especially can make extra work for hosts and their guests, and such accidents cannot always be prevented, even with pouring aids and drip catchers. Red wine stains can be removed by boiling, but delicate fabrics cannot be boiled, since colors may fade or bleed. For this reason, everyone should know how important it is to immediately sprinkle salt on a red wine stain. Salt draws liquids out of fabrics. Even better is to pour mineral water on the spot first; the mineral water will spread the red wine in the weave and the salt can then draw the wine out more easily. What is left of the stain will then disappear in the wash, even on a delicate setting. The same treatment is not recommended for neckties, which cannot be washed. They must be cleaned professionally.

Crystals and Bubbles in Wine

Many white wine lovers are regularly troubled by the presence of small white crystals at the bottom of the bottle. Are they impurities? Undissolved sugar? They are potassium tartrate, also known as argol. These crystals are proof, like the carbon dioxide bubbles found in many white wines, that the wine in question is a quality, rather than a mass-produced, wine.

Argol in an old Sauternes: Enjoyment of the wine is in no way diminished by precipitated potassium tartrate.

Harmless Argol

The potassium tartrate, which looks like sugar crystals or ground glass, has no effect on the taste of a wine. The potassium salt of tartaric acid precipitates out during fermentation or aging of some wines. It can therefore appear in either young white wines or older ones, and is a sign that the wine is "alive." To be sure, you should not drink the argol if it gets into your glass. Cloudiness is to be interpreted in the same way. It suggests that the wine was not stabilized and filtered—a sacrilege for cleanliness fanatics and industrial wine makers. However, quality vintners eschew fining and filtering, since some feel that such practices tend to take away from a wine's individuality.

Carbon Dioxide

People are often troubled by another phenomenon occasionally observed in white wines. Many wines effervesce after serving and develop tiny bubbles in the glass, but this is no cause for panic. The bubbles are merely a remnant of natural carbon dioxide produced during fermentation. Most of it escapes in the barrel (or stainless steel tank), but a small quantity remains dissolved in the wine, even after it has been bottled. It is then released when the bottle is opened. Natural carbon dioxide in a white wine means that the wine is sparkling fresh and lively. It allows the wine drinker to experience the bouquet more intensely, and is therefore desirable. Red wines, by contrast, should not have such effervescence. If a red wine does have bubbles or forms streaks of foam on the surface that do not disappear, the cellar master has neglected to stabilize the wine.

Argol on the Cork: If the wine was stored horizontally, potassium tartrate can build up on the bottom of the cork.

Cloudy White Wine: Suspended particles in white wine are erroneously considered faults. In reality, they are a sign that the wine has not been doctored.

Effervescent White Wine: The carbon dioxide in a wine appears in the form of bubbles that can adhere to the edge of the glass for a long time after pouring.

Foam Streaks: Streaks of foam in red wines suggest that a secondary fermentation has occurred in the bottle, which can have an adverse effect on taste.

TIPS & TRICKS: FIZZY RED WINES

Red wines that effervesce after pouring or form foamy streaks do not have to be poured down the drain. Give them a chance. First, let the wine stand in the glass to see if the bubbles disappear on contact with air. If they do not disappear, the taste of the wine may still be only slightly affected. Or you might try giving the bottle and what wine remains a hefty shaking—after reinserting the cork, of course. A good wine will survive such treatment. If there is still no improvement, let the bottle stand open for a day. If the wine still does not taste right, discard it.

How High to Fill the Glass

One way to demonstrate your lack of familiarity with wine etiquette is to fill your guests' glasses to the rim. You may mean well, but you are really preventing them from enjoying the wine. Glasses filled too full are difficult to hold by the stem, and the wine's bouquet has no chance to develop. Wine also warms up faster in the glass than in the bottle. An overfilled glass also invites gulping rather than savoring.

Rule of Thumb: One-Third Full

As a rule of thumb, small glasses should not be more than a third full. Large glasses may even be only a quarter full. One exception is sparkling-wine glasses, which may be filled almost to the rim. In all other cases you should serve only a small amount, then refill glasses frequently. This is not mere wine snobbery; wine lovers adhere to this practice intuitively. The more expensive the wine, the less they serve—not because they are stingy but because they know that the wine can fully develop only if there is enough room in the glass for the wine to aerate.

The habit of overfilling glasses is nevertheless widespread, especially in restaurants. Servers who fill wineglasses to the top are probably more accustomed to serving beer. They may just as well be pouring the wine into a mug rather than a wineglass. The amount served depends on the glass. Serving a very small amount in a large glass is just as incorrect as filling a small glass to the rim.

Wineglasses correctly filled with sparkling wine, red wine, and white wine.

Correct: Three and a half fluid oz. in the wineglass and five fluid oz. in a quarter-liter pitcher for refilling.

Correct: In a large wineglass, there should be at least seven fluid oz. of wine. A restaurant that offers this much requires the proper glasses.

Tasteless: Seven fluid oz. in a relatively small glass is too much. The wineglass is too heavy, and the bouquet dissipates too quickly.

Ridiculous: Three and a half fluid oz. in a very large glass looks like a puddle. The wine's bouquet will not be able to reach the taster's nose.

TIPS & TRICKS: SEASONING THE GLASS

If you are drinking a second red wine during your meal but have only a single glass, it is necessary to "season" the glass with the new wine to remove the remains of the first one. Pour a small amount of the new wine into the glass, swirl it around, then empty it into the receptacle furnished (or into the glass of your seating partner, who can then repeat the process, passing the "seasoning wine" along). In this manner what is left of the previous wine is eliminated and the aroma of the new one is imparted to the glass. The practice is particularly called for if the new wine comes from an entirely different region or a different vine variety. If it is essentially the same wine and only a different vintage, the process is unnecessary. When switching from a white wine to a red one, a new glass is essential.

How to Hold the Bottle

When asked how to hold the bottle when serving, the English wine writer Cyril Ray tersely replied, "Tightly." But holding a wine bottle tight is not always easy, especially while trying to direct the flow of wine into a glass. The contortions many wine drinkers engage in are ample proof of this.

The correct way to hold any wine bottle—in the center, with the label facing upward.

Stylishly and Securely

A full 750 ml wine bottle weighs about 2.5 pounds (1.25 kg). Holding it properly while serving is therefore not merely a question of etiquette. It is a matter of balancing it in the hand so that the wine flows out in neither a flood nor a dribble. This means grasping it at its center of gravity. This requires little effort and allows you to control the flow of the wine. With a full bottle, the center of gravity is the middle. The emptier the bottle becomes, the lower the center of gravity, and experienced wine drinkers and sommeliers intuitively grasp it lower down. Also, the label should always be uppermost when serving—unless the host has something to hide.

Correct: It is permissible—even essential— to hold magnum bottles with both hands in order to pour the wine safely.

Correct: Squat bottles are held with the flat side up when pouring, the thumb on the label.

Dilettantish: Holding squat bottles vertically is dilettantish. It makes it more difficult to control the flow of the wine.

Klutzy: Grasping wine bottles by the neck is common, but doing so requires more strength and makes it more difficult to control the flow of the wine than when holding the bottle with the proper grip.

Bad Form: Refilling your seating partner's glass is a sign of courtesy, but not if you pour with a backhanded grip on the bottle.

Pretentious: A sommelier may grip a Champagne bottle by the hollow at the bottom. Doing so in your own home is pretentious.

TIPS & TRICKS: SERVING AIDS

When wine is served, there are sometimes spills: unsightly for the guest, upsetting for the host. And even if there are no spills, the last drop frequently runs down the side of the bottle and leaves a red stain on the tablecloth. The solution is a round,

elastic foil called a Drop Stop. Simply curl it with your fingers to form a spout and insert it into the mouth of the bottle. With it you can pour red wine safely, and there are no more drips. It is available in well-stocked wine shops and is inexpensive.

What to Do with Half-Full Bottles

If the wine was good and your guests were robust, there won't be any wine leftover.
But a single person drinking alone is frequently confronted with the problem of
what to do with a half-full bottle. Will what is left still be drinkable the next day?
How can you ensure that it will be?

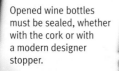

Opened wine bottles
must be sealed, whether
with the cork or with
a modern designer
stopper.

Oxygen—The Enemy

Your wine tasting party has come to an
end. Twisted capsules and corks are lying about. Opened bottles remain on the
table, some still containing wine, now
completely exposed to its worst enemy—
oxygen. Even by the next day wines in
opened bottles can taste stale or even be
completely oxidized, in which case they
have to be poured down the drain.

Young wines have the best protection
against such a fate. They still have a
modicum of free sulfur that bonds with
the oxygen. Tannin also helps protect red
wines from oxidation. Young, tannin-rich
red wines do best at surviving for a day
in an opened bottle. Young Barolos and
Australian Shirazes are often even better the next day. They need air. Fragile,
highly aromatic wines lose their elegance quickly. Old wines that are already
sated with oxygen as a result of aging
and have no more free sulfur are most
likely to lose their flavor once the bottle
has been opened.

Vacuum Pump: This device, sold only in wine shops, draws out the oxygen in the bottle. Many wines will stay fresh longer with it, but the pump is not recommended for old and sensitive wines since the vacuum created can damage the bottle.

Preserver: Sprays with inert gases are best for preserving wine in opened bottles. You simply direct the gas in three brief spurts through the neck of the bottle. The spray is sold only in wine shops and is expensive, but it is enough for eighty applications.

TIPS & TRICKS: WINE FOR COOKING

Wines that are no longer suitable to drink can often be ideal for cooking. A red wine that has lost its freshness from standing open can be used for coq au vin (Burgundies are best) or a delicious red-wine butter. Even if the wine is already slightly oxidized, it can still be used in sauces. In any case, its delicate aromas are lost after simmering for hours. With leftover white wines, you can create delicate aspics. Sweet wines make wonderful jellies for pork and liver dishes. Champagne and other sparkling wines are ideal in seafood risotto.

The "Sisi" Method: Named after Empress Elisabeth of Austria, this method preserves the carbon dioxide at least for a time. You simply hang the handle of a silver teaspoon in the neck of the bottle. A barrier of coolness is produced around the metal that reduces the flight of the carbon dioxide.

Bargas: In a variant on the Empress's method, a wedge of stainless steel is suspended in an open sparkling wine bottle. An Italian invention, it slows down the escape of carbon dioxide and the attendant loss of pressure in the bottle. The wedge must not come in contact with the wine.

Proper Temperatures for Serving Wine

Drinking fine wines too warm or too cool is almost as bad as serving them in a coffee cup. The proper temperature is just as important as a suitable glass. Since not all wine drinkers have a cool cellar for white wines and a slightly warmer one for red wines, they must make do with other methods. You may want to consider purchasing a wine thermometer.

Temperature Helps

The most important instrument for checking wine temperature is a wine thermometer. Simply place it in the wine glass, and it will indicate the wine's precise temperature. It is easy enough to use one at home, but hardly appropriate to reach for one at someone else's house or in a restaurant. There are also thermometers that you place around the bottle like a cuff. They have the advantage of measuring temperature without having to open the bottle, but of course they tell you the temperature of the bottle only, not of its contents. The two can differ markedly. If a bottle has been placed in a bucket of ice cubes for a short time, the glass of the bottle may be chilled but the contents may still be near room temperature.

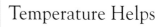

Red wines that have been served too cool can be warmed a few degrees by cradling them in your hands.

Wine Thermometer: An indispensable instrument for checking a wine's temperature, but one that should be used only in your home.

Clay Wine Cooler: Hold the cooler under cold water, then place the previously chilled bottle inside. Evaporation creates a protective layer of cold around the bottle.

Double-Walled Acrylic Cooler: The cushion of coolness that the chilled bottle builds up around it slows the warming of the wine.

Country of Origin	Drinking Temperature for White and Red Wines						
	42°F (6°C)	46°F (8°C)	50°F (10°C)	54°F (12°C)	58°F (14°C)	62°F (16°C)	66°F (18°C)
France	Vin de Pays Rosé	Champagne Bourgogne Blanc Sancerre Saumur Muscadet Chablis Bordeaux Sec Rosé de Provence	Pouilly Fumé Chablis Grand Cru Meursault Gewürztraminer Riesling Grand Cru Tavel Rosé Lirac Rosé de Provence Sauternes (sweet)	Puligny-Montrachet Montrachet Corton-Charlemagne Musigny Blanc Tokay d'Alsace	Vin de Pays Beaujolais Primeur	Vin de Pays Mercury Mâcon Rouge Chinon Beaujolais Cru all Burgundies Bordeaux Superieur Madiran Côtes-du-Rhône	Médoc, Haut Médoc, Pauillac, Margaux, St.-Emilion, Pomerol, Graves, Cahors, Côtes de Languedoc, Côtes de Roussillon, Côtes de Provence, Châteauneuf-du-Pape, Côte-Rôtie, Hermitage
Italy	Prosecco Frizzante Galestro Pinot Grigio	Prosecco Spumante South Tirol wines Chardonnay (without wood) Soave Gavi Arneis	Chardonnay Barrique Verdicchio Friuli white wines	Marsala Vin Santo	Lago di Caldaro Valpolicella Bardolino Lambrusco	Chianti Vino Nobile Rosso di Montalcino Barbera d'Alba Merlot del Piave Pinot Nero South Tirol Lagrein Cabernet Friaul Sangiovese di Romagna Valtellina Rosso	Chianti Riserva Brunello di Montalcino Aglianico di Vulture Taurasi Barbera d'Asti Barbaresco Barolo Amarone South Tirol Merlot
Germany	QbA sweet Weissherbst Vintner Sekt	QbA/Kabinett Vintage or Vineyard Sekt	Spätlese/ Auslese trocken Beerenauslese	Grauburgunder Auslese	Trollinger	Spätburgunder Dornfelder Lemberger	
Austria	G'spritzter	Grüner Veltliner Riesling Welschriesling Neuburger	Ausbruch Beerenauslese	Smaragd Wachau Sauvignon Steiermark		Blauer Zweigelt St. Laurent	Blaufränkisch
Switzerland		Fendant, Aigle Epesses	Œil de Perdrix			Blauburgunder Dôle	Merlot del Ticino
Spain	Rosado	Albariño Cava		Sherry		Valdepeñas	Rioja, Ribera del Duero, Tinto Navarra, Priorato
Portugal	Vinho Verde				Port Madeira	Ribatejo	Alentejo, Dão, Bairrado
New World	White Zinfandel	Sauvignon Blanc	Fumé Blanc	Chardonnay Barrique		Pinot Noir	Cabernet Sauvignon, Zinfandel, Shiraz, Pinotage, Malbec

Chilling White Wine

White wine stored at room temperature in an apartment is generally too warm. Rapidly bringing it down to serving temperature is called chilling. An ice bucket is an especially effective method. Ice water helps maintain a cool temperature.

Serving Temperature

Because a wine warms quickly in the glass, it is necessary to serve it a few degrees cooler than the ideal drinking temperature. A professional, therefore, distinguishes between serving and drinking temperatures. This means that wines that have the proper drinking temperature are briefly placed in an ice bath so that they may be served a few degrees cooler. It is a problem when guests appear unexpectedly at the door with a sparkling wine that was stored in their kitchen at room temperature and it must be quickly cooled to 54°F (12°C). Well aware that rapid chilling is a shock for any wine and that its quality may suffer as a result, inventive sommeliers have come up with a relatively gentle chilling method.

The Ice Bath

The ice bucket is an indispensable but dangerous utensil for the wine lover. Indispensable because chilled wines grow warmer, especially in summer, and should be put on ice at least for a bit to preserve the proper serving temperature. Dangerous because the ice bucket cools wines very rapidly—especially if the bottle is only half full. Within fifteen minutes white wines and Champagne sink, in an ice bath to 46°F (8°C), and are thus too cold to drink. Taking the bottle out in time is just as important as placing it there in the first place.

An ice bucket is an indispensable tool for all who like to drink their white wines chilled.

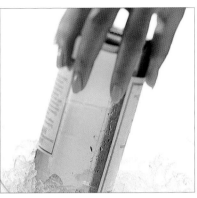

Rapid Chilling: Place the unopened bottle upside down in ice water. The temperature drops faster in the neck of the bottle and the shoulder area than in the middle of the bottle.

Speeding Up: After five minutes, briefly agitate the bottle in the bucket, then turn it in the ice right side up. In this way, the slightly cooled wine from the middle of the bottle comes into contact with the cold bottle wall.

Further Cooling: After another five minutes, remove the bottle from the ice water and carefully open it. The first four glasses will have a temperature of roughly 54°F (12°C). Return the bottle to the ice bucket, this time with the neck facing up. The wine in the belly of the bottle continues to chill.

Serving Temperature

With Champagne (or other sparkling wines), the ice bucket has yet another function: The cold helps to keep the carbon dioxide in them longer. As long as they are on ice, opened sparkling wines continue to be effervescent.

Time in Minutes	Desired Serving Temperature (in °F)						
	58°	56°	54°	52°	50°	48°	46,
77°	183	219	245	287	378	472	612
75°	159	188	220	272	351	457	589
73°	139	173	208	259	334	430	561
72°	117	158	197	249	310	399	539
70°	98	133	178	235	302	382	518
68°	83	123	164	220	292	369	502
66°	72	102	149	201	275	358	486
64°	57	82	117	175	234	329	466
63°	39	66	95	140	221	315	448
61°	25	46	76	109	170	278	378
59°	20	28	53	88	127	225	335
58°	0	24	33	63	104	174	273

Beginning Temperature (in °F)

Cooling time (in minutes) that a white wine at various temperatures requires in the refrigerator to attain the desired serving temperature.

TIPS & TRICKS: CRUSHED ICE

Making ice cubes for the wine cooler in the freezer is a tedious business. It is simpler to make a block of ice in a rectangular casserole, for example, or a 10-quart (10-liter) freezer bag placed in a cardboard box. Whenever you need ice, wrap the block in a dishcloth and break it up with a hammer. The ice quickly shatters and can be easily shaken into the bucket in the cloth.

Warming Red Wine

Red wines generally come out of the cellar too cool. Generally, warming a wine is done by fetching the bottle from the cellar a few hours before opening it and placing it in a warmer space. But take care: Living rooms are warmer than they used to be, and room temperature is not drinking temperature. Sometimes red wines that have become too warm have to be put in the refrigerator for a short time.

Time in Minutes	Serving and Drinking Temperature for Red Wine (in °F)							
Cellar Temperature (in °F)	58°	59°	61°	63°	64°	66°	68°	
46°	39	57	80	105	131	162	195	Time (in minutes) that a wine needs to warm from cellar temperature to the desired serving temperature (given a standard room temperature of 70°F [21°C]).
48°	36	54	77	102	128	159	190	
50°	33	51	74	99	125	155	187	
52°	28	46	69	94	120	150	182	
54°	20	38	61	86	112	142	174	
56°	15	33	54	79	105	135	167	
58°	0	18	41	66	92	122	154	
59°		0	23	48	74	104	136	
61°			0	25	51	81	113	
63°				0	26	56	88	
64°					0	30	62	

Timing

The table is set. The candles are lit. The crystal glasses sparkle. And the wine was brought up from the cellar earlier and stands ready. Then suddenly you wonder if it is the right serving temperature. If it is, how do you keep it from warming too much before the guests arrive? Is it too warm? Clearly you may have to warm or chill it further. The above table shows how long a red wine needs to warm to the desired serving temperature.

Frequently, red wine that comes from the cellar has to be warmed to bring it up to the proper drinking temperature.

Warm-Water Bath: With a water temperature of 86°F (30°C), a red wine takes only 30 minutes to warm from 58°F (14°C) to 66°F (18°C) — old-fashioned but gentle.

Red Wine on the Radiator or the Stove: The way your grandfather did it. The wine at the base of the bottle warms rapidly, while that near the shoulder remains cool. Barbaric.

Microwave: A reckless warming method, since microwaves can damage the wine and the rise in temperature is virtually uncontrollable. Catastrophic.

Cooling Sleeve: The sleeve, which is filled with a gel, must be chilled in the freezer compartment before you place it around the bottle. A gentle method.

Ice Bucket: Rapid cooling that modern red wines tolerate with aplomb. In less than 20 minutes, a warm wine is chilled to serving temperature. Easy method.

Freezing Compartment: Shock cooling, but since 10 minutes are enough to bring a wine from room temperature down to drinking temperature (66°F [18°C]), this is a tolerable method; there is no damage to the wine.

Decanting Red Wine

The careful transfer of wine from the bottle to a carafe is called "decanting." Many people find this practice affected. Others even warn against it. In fact, decanting makes sense only with a few wines. Young, tannin-rich red wines improve in taste thanks to the aeration. Old red wines can be separated from any sediment in the bottle by decanting.

With this decanting scale, an old wine can be ceremoniously separated from its sediment. Generally, however, a wine steward decants by hand.

The Reason for Decanting

Decanting is nothing more than a controlled oxygen shock for the wine. Acids, esters, and hydrocarbon molecules (which contain important taste carriers) rapidly combine with oxygen, thereby allowing the flavor of the wine to "unfold." This rapid unfolding is hindered in the bottle by tannin. Tannin reacts more readily with oxygen than with other substances and binds to it—which is normally desirable. This protects the wine from rapid spoilage. Tannin-rich wines unfold more slowly. The wine can age longer. But if the wine is drunk early, the unfolding of the wine has to be assisted—by decanting.

The Decanting Scale

The decanting scale is an English invention. The device was once used for decanting Port wines. Older vintage Port forms a heavy sediment. By turning the handle you can adjust the angle of the bottle precisely. The lighted candle under the neck of the bottle helps you see when the sediment begins to flow through, at which point you stop decanting so that the sediment stays in the bottle. These days, decanting scales are used for ceremonial purposes, and when they are used, it is not only for Port but also for older red wines.

Decanting Basket: Old red wines are served in a basket not just for show but so sediment can settle. The last of the wine stays in the bottle along with the deposit.

Decanting Funnel: With a funnel you can pour the wine from the bottle into a carafe without a candle. The sediment is caught in the sieve.

TIPS & TRICKS: DRINKING THE SEDIMENT IN BURGUNDIES

Aubert de Villaine, director and co-owner of the Domaine de la Romanée-Conti in Burgundy, recommends that you drink the sediment of a valuable old Burgundy—even though it looks unattractive. It tastes sweet, not bitter. The reason: Sediment in some Burgundies is flaky, not granular. The flakes are not precipitated tannin (Burgundy is not an especially tannin-rich wine) but rather pigments (polyphenoles). The effect is recognizable with the naked eye; the color of a 20-year-old wine is nearly coffee-brown. Moreover, the flakes swirl around even at the slightest movement of the bottle. Those who decant old Burgundies can easily lose a third of the bottle's contents—a waste of a noble wine.

Decanting Technique: Wines that need to be decanted because of their sediment should stand upright for 24 hours before serving. The sediment needs time to become dislodged from the wall of the bottle and settle to the bottom. When decanting over a candle, watch to see when the sediment begins to flow out. It takes the form of a thin, grainy streak.

Decanting White Wine

While decanting red wines is common enough, the notion of decanting white wines has fallen out of favor. In the nineteenth century, it was altogether expected that you would serve a worthy white wine in a carafe. Today, more people are recognizing that aeration can be just as beneficial to specific white wines as to certain reds.

A Practice Revived

The idea of decanting white wines was recently revived in Austria. The Wachau vintners Franz Hirzberger and Emmerich Knoll were always puzzled to note that the third glass of a Riesling Smaragd or a Grüner Veltliner Smaragd tasted better than the first. The solution: The wine in the third glass had had more time to react to the oxygen in the opened bottle. Thus, it seemed fuller and more harmonious. Sommeliers have had similar experiences with high-quality white wines from Alsace, Germany, and Burgundy. Only after they had stood for an hour or two in a carafe could their fullness and multi-faceted richness be fully appreciated.

An old tradition revived: High-quality white wines are decanted so that their bouquet can fully develop.

Breathing in the Glass: A glass with an adequate diameter can come close to the decanter effect. It lets the wine breathe.

False: Large carafes are not suited for the decanting of white wine. The surface in contact with the air is too great.

White Wines for Decanting: Grüner Veltliner Smaragd, a white Burgundy *grand cru*, an Alsatian Riesling *grand cru*.

TIPS & TRICKS: CLEANING CARAFES

Many carafes tend to develop a film on the inside of the glass after repeated use. Normal detergents do not generally remove it. But if you let vinegar work on it for a few hours, the coating generally disappears. Afterward, rinse out the carafe several times, then let it dry on a decanter stand. These are available in mail-order shops that sell wine accessories. If you have no decanter carafe but wish to decant a wine, you can use an old trick: carefully decant the wine into a mineral-water bottle, then pour it back into the original bottle.

Choosing the Right Glass

Experienced wine drinkers say that the most important thing about a wineglass is that it be open at the top. There's no disputing this idea, of course, but there are some other qualities worth mentioning. First, a wineglass for epicures has little in common with a wineglass for tipplers. Second, the better the wine, the more important it is that you use the right glass.

Form and Function

An elegant wineglass must be transparent and thin. You should be able to feel the temperature of the wine with your lips. The edge should be cut thin so that the wine flows directly onto the tongue and not past it. A good wineglass should have a stem that allows you to lift it safely to your mouth. Its center of gravity should be such that it balances nicely in your hand and is easy to drink from.

Qualities to avoid? Neither the stem, the foot, nor the bowl should be colored. Colored glass distorts the color of the wine. Also, the bowl should not be too small. It should be able to hold at least three times the amount actually served, for only then can a wine fully develop in the glass. On the other hand, the bowl should not be too large. Drinking mediocre wines out of monstrous glasses is ridiculous. Simple wines taste better when served in bistro glasses. Just as distressing are hand-crafted glasses of ornamental pressed glass with thick stems.

If you drink good wines you need good glasses. They do not have to be expensive, simply functional.

TIPS & TRICKS: WASHING WINEGLASSES

Almost all wineglasses can be safely washed in a dishwasher. But frequently they don't fit because of their long stems and must be washed by hand. It is best to use only hot water. To remove traces of lipstick or grease from the rim, you may have to add a little detergent to the water. After washing, rinse the glasses with clean water and immediately dry them with a cloth rather than letting them drain. There is a microfiber cloth developed especially for glassware that leaves no streaks available in some wine shops. Linen is just as good, for it does not leave any lint. But to make a linen towel absorbent, you have to put it through the washing machine ten times.

Examples of Bad Taste: In times when wine was drunk only on special occasions, wineglasses often stood in the dining room cabinet waiting to be used. Perhaps that was just as well. Of course, you could drink wine from them, but perhaps not enjoy it. Even good wines could pale in wineglasses like these.

1 German Römer with a heavy colored stem. Distorts the color of the wine, and the bowl does not permit development of the bouquet. **2** A thick, decorative glass without a stem requires that you grasp it by the bowl. **3** Copy of an Alsatian Riesling glass with a brown stem—more of a cup than a wineglass. **4** A kitschy glass with trapped air bubbles; the thick glass and the trumpet-shaped bowl rob the wine of all aroma and taste. **5** Pressed glass with a trunk instead of a stem; the wine has no chance to develop. **6** Wineglass made from cut glass: the flared rim causes the wine to enter the mouth in a broad stream, so that it passes the tastebuds and rapidly drains down the throat.

Sparkling Wine Straight

Sparkling wines are frequently mixed with fruit juices or other drinks. The result is a fizz cocktail, a tingling, thirst-quenching drink in which the taste of wine is lost. Sekt, cava, and Prosecco are especially well suited for cocktails. But what about

The Black Velvet is an undisputed classic among sparkling wine cocktails.

Black Velvet

One of the most famous and most controversial Champagne cocktails is the Black Velvet. It was developed in the London club Buck' Fizz in the 1930s. Bartenders filled their guests' glasses half full of Guinness stout and then slowly topped them with Champagne. The marriage of beer and Champagne elicited violent controversy. Purists found it tasteless and vulgar, but Englishmen liked the mix and scolded their critics for being snobs. Cyril Ray, a wine expert and author of a monograph on the Bollinger Champagne house, dryly commented that he did not share the snobbish view that Guinness and Champagne don't mix. But for a Black Velvet, he would not recommend a Champagne from Bollinger. In any case, the Black Velvet continues to be served at some of the world's best bars. The only difference is that now the percentage of Guinness has diminished to three tablespoons per glass.

Mimosa

The most famous cocktail that uses wine is the Mimosa—one part fresh-squeezed orange juice topped with two parts Champagne. To be sure, you wouldn't use a prestige cuvée or a valuable vintage Champagne, but any inexpensive sparkling wine will do. Nowadays, people even use orange juice made from concentrate rather than fresh-squeezed.

or Cocktail Fizz?

Champagne? Does it always have to be drunk "straight," or can it too be used in a fizz? Fizzes are permissible, and there are astonishing combinations, even though purists shake their heads at them.

Cava and Prosecco

What makes sparkling wines so suitable for cocktails is carbon dioxide. It intensifies the flavor of whatever is added and refreshes the palate. But it is important that additions be sparing. No cocktail should have more than one and a half oz. (6 cl) of added ingredients. The basic winy note must be preserved. Sparkling wine cocktails should never be mixed in a shaker; the violent shaking destroys the effervescence. It is a myth that Champagne is especially well suited for use in cocktails; Prosecco and cava serve the same purpose—Sekt too, provided it is not too aromatic.

Starlight: Herbal liqueur, Champagne, half an apricot. An old Hollywood classic in which Prosecco is generally used rather than Champagne.

Campari-Prosecco: Campari and Prosecco. For decades, this has awakened new life in tired spirits.

Blue Champagne: Lemon juice, blue Curaçao, Champagne. Epicures drink this Caribbean-blue cocktail with Champagne, hardcore drinkers with vodka.

Mimosa: Fresh-squeezed orange juice, Champagne, sugar cube. For all those who find straight Champagne too dry and orange juice alone too healthy.

Kir Royal: Champagne and cassis liqueur. Invented on the French Riviera and now a cult cocktail in Germany.

Bellini: Prosecco, pureed peach, apricot brandy. An Italian cocktail that set out on its world conquest from Harry's Bar in Venice.

A Brief Primer for Wine Drinkers

"Wine is the most civilized thing in the world," Ernest Hemingway wrote while gazing at a radiant Margaux. That wine must be drunk differently than whiskey was clear to him. There have always been rules about the consumption of fine wine. But many such rules are merely ceremonious, some being nothing but fossilized etiquette. It is worth learning a few of these rules, even though they may seem artificial and anything but natural to a beginner. Breaking these rules is no catastrophe, but lapses may upset some people.

Posture and Pleasure

Wine is not drunk. It is savored in tiny sips. You sometimes hear the phrase "mouthful of wine," but you shouldn't take it literally. It's a metaphor used to describe an especially hearty, animated wine. When tasting, you should raise your arm to lift the glass to your mouth—a simple, but by no means obvious rule. Some wine drinkers appear to forget themselves and, already on their second glass, no longer lift their arm. Instead, they sit with elbows on the table and lean over the glass—a depressing sight, even though there is no arguing that the wine ultimately ends up where it is supposed to.

When the wine leaves the glass, it first touches the upper lip and is then carefully drawn into the mouth through open lips. This motion may seem forced, but it is in reality a highly natural, uncramped procedure for enjoyment. Much more strain is involved—not to say boorishness—in throwing back your head as though drinking out of a beer mug and letting the wine flow into a wide-open mouth. Such a pose betrays the type of the competitive drinker you generally encounter in beer gardens.

Moreover, the wine should not be swallowed immediately, but briefly "weighed" on the tongue. This allows it to develop its full flavor. Demonstratively "chewing" the wine is suitable at wine tastings, but at table it is generally considered déclassé. The wineglass does not have to be set down after each sip. It is perfectly acceptable to hold it in your hand and take a second sip after the first one has cleared your throat. But anyone who takes two or three gulps one after another does not appear to be a true appreciator of wine. People who take long, deep swallows and then sit there with flushed cheeks, obviously having difficulty savoring the wine, only come across as boorish. Those who are drinking to satisfy thirst should not be drinking wine in the first place; mineral water is a much better idea. A glass should never be held by the bowl but rather by the stem—if it has one. Simple country wines are often drunk from small mugs with handles and can at times even be thirst-quenching.

The wine is drawn into the mouth with the lips, in small quantities.

Throwing back your head and tossing the wine down—the posture of the competitive drinker.

Correct: Small glasses can easily be lifted to your mouth with two fingers without losing balance.

Correct: Three fingers are used for red wineglasses with large bowls to hold them securely.

Correct: It is often necessary to use four fingers to hold a heavy wineglass securely.

Déclassé: Holding a wineglass by the base is something left to cellar masters, and possibly wine testers. In social situations, it looks undignified and out of place.

Unaesthetic: Grasping the bowl of the wine-glass with your whole hand is inelegant. The fingers leave unattractive prints on the glass.

Affected: The raised little finger does not detract from your enjoyment of the wine, but betrays a desire for artifice.

WINE TALK

Wine has a language all its own, but individual wine drinkers tend to have their own favorite terms. With their comments—whether of delight or rejection—they reveal themselves as one of the following types.

The Pleasant Bore: *pleasant, decent, full-mouthed, typical of the type, pure-toned, flowery, racy, round, firm, lasting, appealing.*

The Wine Rambo: *lusty stuff, super stuff, sexy, wicked tannin, crazy taste, hellish elderberry bouquet, pomegranate wine, explosive force, monumental, titanic, gigantic.*

The Unimaginative Expert: *complex, many-layered, good structure, medium body, smooth length, well-integrated acid.*

The Frustrated Writer: *"All hell is loose on the palate." "This wine is like a kick in the stomach." "Delicate as the bite of a young viper." "Smells like the sweat of angels."*

The Unapproachable Expert: *seedy tannin, balanced astringency, fine sandy texture, yellow fruit, superficial malolactic, horsy terroir note.*

The Arty Expert: *"Like a Bach fugue." "As voluptuous as a Rubens nude." "Gay as a Mozart minuet." "The bouquet seems gone with the wind."*

The Modern Wine Nerd: *tasty, really delicious, chic, right.*

Wine and Its Aromas

Wine is the most varied aromatic product of nature Not everyone has a sense for its subtleties. But for everyone it can be rewarding to sharpen that sense. "They teach us to read, write, and do arithmetic. Why not to smell?" asks the French aroma researcher Jean Lenoir.

Wine Taste and Aroma

Chemically, wine is a mixture of water, alcohol, and various acids and their by-products. These basic substances can enter into myriad combinations, and this is enough to give the wine a preciou aroma. "Tasting wine is the basis for the enjoyment of wine," wrote Emile Peynaud, Professor of Oenology at the University of Bordeaux.

Aroma Sensations

Aroma and taste are wine's most important sensory stimuli. Aldehyde, esters, and ketones are responsible for aromas. But only a small minority of these aromatic substances actually smell, namely the volatile ones. Scientists have isolated roughly 800 such compounds and can identify them precisely. Methoxy-2-isobutyl-3-pyrazin, for example, is a molecule that is often present in the Chinon wines of the Loire and gives them their characteristic strong note of green peppers. But the "green peppers" sensation is only a mental association. The molecule in question is not present in every pepper. For that reason, not everyone associates green peppers with a Vouvray, a Saumur, a Coulée-de-Serrant, or one of the many other Chinon wines. The plum aroma by which blindfolded experts can identify a ripe Burgundy wine is not present at all in an actual plum. That is to say the molecule in the wine that gives rise to plum associations does not exist in the fruit.

Swirling the wine in the glass intensifies its bouquet.

Complexity of Taste

Conversely, analysis identifies many aromatic compounds in wine that are not perceptible to the sense organs. Their concentrations are so slight that they lie below our perception threshold. This is especially true of an aroma, although the mucous membrane is a much more sensitive organ than the tongue. Most of what people taste they actually smell. The taste of a wine depends on only a few basic substances, specifically the alcohol and the acids present in the wine. They determine whether a wine tastes sweet or bitter, sour or salty.

Smelling and Tasting

In addition, people's sense organs are not all equally perceptive. One person registers scents that another does not perceive at all. To enjoy wine, it is therefore necessary to concentrate. That does not mean you have to meditate over every sip. Perceiving the aroma is easier, for example, if you briefly swirl the wine around in the glass, then smell it. The additional contact with air strengthens the aroma. But be careful, because it is easy to swirl so hard that the wine splashes out. If you are not confident about swirling wine, do not swirl the glass in your hand but on the table.

The taste of a wine is intensified by "weighing" and "chewing" it on the tongue. This forces the wine to flood the tongue's papillae and stimulate them. When tasting wine, it may be necessary to noisily suck in a gasp of air, even though doing so may seem inappropriate in public.

Studying the Wine: White wines should always be completely clear and transparent. Red wines should have no cloudiness beyond any possible sediment.

Legs on the Glass: A number of "tears" or "legs" on the side of the glass mean that it is a full-bodied, alcohol-rich wine.

The Smell Test: This tells more about the quality of the wine than the taste test. All faults, as well as the wine's taste peculiarities, are communicated in the aroma.

The Attack: The first contact of the wine with the tongue is called the attack. The fruit sugar is perceived above all and registered as pleasant or unpleasant.

"Chewing" the Wine: Chewing tells you whether a wine "stops behind the teeth" or offers more complex aromas, delicate tannins, and greater depth.

The Finish: Only after swallowing is it apparent how long a wine resonates. Experts speak of a short or long finish.

The Various Wine Aromas

The taste of wine is composed of many different aromas. The wine drinker does not perceive them individually but rather only the overall taste of the wine, and from it forms a taste image. Distinguishing the individual aromas and being able to name them is the height of degustation.

"Le Nez du Vin"

The Frenchman Jean Lenoir, a vintner's son, has worked for many years to capture the aromas of wine and preserve them in sniffing bottles. With them, all who wish to practice winetasting can learn to distinguish aromas such as grapefruit, walnuts, green peppers, leather, or toasted bread. He has collected 54 typical wine aromas in his aroma compendium "Le Nez du Vin." As is customary in France, Lenoir distinguishes between primary, secondary, and even tertiary aromas.

Primary and Secondary Aromas

The French identify as primary aromas those typical of the vine variety—floral, fruity, or spicy notes that are already found in the grapes and later reappear in the wine. Bouquet substances that appear during fermentation are called secondary aromas. These too are fruity and spicy notes; however, they are aromas not found in the grapes but rather produced during the fermentation process.

Tertiary Aromas

All aging aromas are considered to be tertiary aromas. These are aromas created by aging that takes place in the barrel and in the bottle, where fruity and spicy molecules break down and recombine with others. New aroma sensations are developed in this way. Many seem unusual, some even bizarre. But what may sound strange can taste delicious, even wonderful, in the wine. The wine's quality depends on how rich, varied, and complex its aroma is. A high-quality wine always has many secondary and tertiary aromas, while primary aromas alone cause a wine to seem one-dimensional. This classification makes it easier to judge the quality of a wine.

"Le Nez du Vin" contains 54 sniffing vials containing various wine aromas.

Primary Aromas	Secondary Aromas	Tertiary Aromas
Lime	Honey	Dried fruit
Grapefruit	Litchi	Marmalade
Acacia blossoms	Quince	Raisins
Violets	Pear	Port wine
Roses	Pineapple	Cloves
Cherries	Papaya	Olive oil
Black currants	Mango	Cocoa
Raspberries	Banana	Chocolate
Cranberries	Walnut	Coffee beans
Blackberries	Butter	Cedar wood
Grass	Bread crust (yeast)	Sweet gum
Stinging nettle	Saffron	Vanilla
Green asparagus	Black pepper	Leather polish
Green pepper		Caramel
		Tar
		Licorice
		Mushrooms
		Moss (forest floor)
		Tobacco

Wine Faults and Other Irritations

Corkiness is the best-known wine fault. But there are many other flaws that can detract from the enjoyment of a wine. The causes are almost always mistakes made during a wine's production or storage. Some faults may be resolved after the fact. Others are not actual faults, disappearing later by themselves.

Wine Down the Drain

For faulty wines there is nothing to do but pour them out. They are not even suitable for cooking. This is especially true of wines with a corky taste, which make up the majority of faulty wines. Officially, only 1 percent of wines are corky, but the actual figure lies between 3 and 8 percent —and is increasing, as many wine dealers will attest. Other wine faults are less common. The findings of modern wine-science have changed many methods of wine production from the ground up. Carefully timing and rapid harvesting,

THE 11 MOST COMMON WINE FAULTS

Reduction Bouquet
Chemical Substance: Sulfur, hydrogen sulfide, mercaptans, thiols, sulfides.
Aroma/taste: Sweat, mustiness, soap, horse stable, apothecary cupboard.
Cause: Typical by-products of fermentation that normally disappear during aeration after racking (or separation from the must) but can still linger in the finished wine and only appear on the opening of the bottle.
Diagnosis: Not a wine fault.
Where encountered: Typical of young red wines, which on opening smell distinctly, even unpleasantly astringent.
Treatment: Decant the wine, let the bottle stand open for half an hour, or let the wine stand in the glass for ten minutes.

Staleness
Chemical substance: Acetaldehyde.
Aroma/taste: Staleness, odor of rotten apples, in red wine an aroma of chamomile.
Cause: The young wine had too much contact with oxygen, either in the transfer from one barrel to another or during bottling. Acetaldehyde can also result from insufficient sulfuring. Often the consumer is responsible for the staleness, having left a wine bottle open for a day or more.
Diagnosis: Diminishes the quality of the wine more or less definitively, but still not recognized by many as a wine fault.
Where encountered: Can occur in either white wines or red wines.
Treatment: No treatment.

Oxidation
Chemical substance: Ethyl acetate.
Aroma/taste: Extreme staleness, aroma of walnuts or Madeira, rancid.
Cause: Almost wholly the result of insufficient sulfurization in the cellar, so that the oxygen oxidizes certain aroma components in the wine.
Diagnosis: In its early stage it is called mellowness, later simply oxidation. Once it reaches the latter, the wine must be discarded.
Where encountered: Rarely met with in young wines—more common in old wines in which the supply of free sulfuric acids has already been disintegrated over the years.
Treatment: No treatment. Opened wines also oxidize quickly.

Barrel Tone
Chemical substances: Ethyl fenchol and others.
Aroma/taste: Decay, damp earth, mildew.
Cause: When wine barrels stand empty and are not washed with hot water and natrium carbonate before refilling, molds that settle in the cracks can damage the wine.
Diagnosis: Faulty. If the barrel tone is only faint, the wine can still be enjoyed. Otherwise, it needs to be discarded.
Where encountered: Predominantly in red wines. Inadequate barrel hygiene can be found in both large cellars and small ones.
Treatment: The musty barrel tone never disappears from the wine.

Volatile Acids
Chemical substance: Ethyl acetate.
Aroma/taste: Nail-polish remover, shellac, solvents, glue.
Cause: Excess acetic acid is produced by too rapid fermentation at too high temperatures. It is the most important volatile acid in the wine. Once the wine comes into contact with oxygen after the bottle is opened, it immediately dissipates.
Diagnosis: In a concentration of 1.2 grams per liter you can definitely taste the acid; above 1.5 grams it constitutes a fault. Wine drinkers of different continents react differently to volatile acids.
Where encountered: In both red and white wines.
Treatment: Volatile acid is more likely tolerated in heavy, alcohol-rich red wines than in light white wines.

Lactic Acid Tone
Chemical substance: Diacetyl.
Aroma/taste: Smells like milk powder, whey, sometimes even sauerkraut.
Cause: Insufficient sulfurization after alcoholic fermentation. That is to say that the lactic acid bacteria that cause the biological decomposition of acids continue to be active and produce, in addition to lactic acid, other by-products, such as diacetyl.
Diagnosis: The diagnosis varies. A slight lactic acid tone spoils the pure taste of the wine. A real bite of lactic acid means that the wine cannot be used.

immediate delivery and processing of grapes, controlled fermentation temperatures, the availability of pure cultivated yeasts, better hygiene in the cellar—all have greatly reduced the appearance of excessive acetic acid, sour-milk tones, mercaptan and overoaked tones. Cellar masters are, as a rule, better trained than they used to be, and winemaking techniques are more sophisticated. Also, wine drinkers are more demanding. Stale oxidized wines were a constant annoyance in many parts of Europe twenty years ago, but this is much less the case today. Competition in the wine market is intense, and wine drinkers now readily compare one wine with another.

Unique Note or Fault?

By no means can every unusual taste be called a flaw. The composition of the soil and the climate leave their mark even in high-quality wines, and some of these, whether from the Rhône or Sardinia, from Spain's Estramadura or Bordeaux, can exhibit unusual flavors. Such tones enrich a wine's aroma; they are what distinguish it from all other wines. Demanding wine drinkers even search out wines with distinctive taste profiles. Unique tastes and faults are sometimes closely related.

Where encountered: Mostly met with in white wines.
Treatment: Generally the wine is irreparably spoiled.

Mousiness
Chemical substances: Brettanomyces and Dekkera yeasts.
Aroma/taste: Smells astringent and metallic, often of the cow stall, manure.
Cause: A specific family of yeasts not uncommon in vineyards, the Brettanomyces, gives the wine a foul tone if they are not rendered harmless by sulfuring.
Diagnosis: Not a definite wine fault. Modern wine drinkers are more often offended by the aroma than wine drinkers centuries ago.
Where encountered: Appears almost exclusively in red wines.
Treatment: Tolerable in small doses, otherwise anything but delicate.

Sulfur
Chemical substance: Sulfur dioxide.
Aroma/taste: Smells like burning matches, slightly tingling or biting in the nose.
Cause: Over-sulfuring.
Diagnosis: Wine fault.
Where encountered: Generally appears in white wines and can distort the whole bouquet. Rarely in red wines, as they are less heavily sulfured.
Treatment: The smell of sulfur can be moderated by aerating the wine while decanting.

Mercaptan
Chemical substance: Hydrogen sulfide.
Aroma/taste: Rotten eggs, skunk, onions, garlic, cauliflower.
Cause: The causes are many. The releasing substance is always hydrogen sulfide, which can form under a shortage of nitrogen by either specific yeasts, overly warm fermentation, or the use of certain fungicides in the vineyard. If the hydrogen sulfide is not removed by the cellar master after fermentation, it reacts with alcohol and forms ethyl mercaptans, which then produce the foul-smelling aromas.
Diagnosis: Wine fault.
Where encountered: Now relatively rare.
Treatment: Once the wine is bottled, there is no way to eliminate the problem.

Corkiness
Chemical substance: Trichloranisol.
Aroma/taste: Musty, stale, moldy.
Cause: Comes from the metabolic products of molds that were not killed when the cork rind was disinfected.
Diagnosis: Wine fault.
Where encountered: In recent years, this has become more common—found in from 3 to 8 percent of wines sealed with cork.
Treatment: No treatment possible.

Corkiness is the most common wine fault. Often the cork itself smells musty.

Woodiness
Aroma/taste: Intensely sweet vanilla, toasted wood, fresh sawdust.
Cause: Comes from too long storage of the wine in small, new oak casks (barriques), also from too heavy scorching of barrels before they are used.
Diagnosis: Not a wine fault, but definitely reduces quality. The natural aroma of the wine is masked, as it smells and tastes only of wood. Tolerance for the smell of new wood varies from country to country and between wine drinkers.
Where encountered: Often in non-European wines.
Treatment: No treatment possible.

Super-Tasters and Non-Tasters

Do some people have a more sensitive tongue than others? Are there those who have no sense of taste at all, for whom the world of wine aromas is wholly inaccessible? Are the abilities to smell and to taste innate? This much is certain: Sense organs are developed to different degrees in different people. Yet if some taste less, it is not always the fault of the sense organ.

What Do We Taste, Where, and How

The palate, the mouth cavity, and the tongue are dotted with several thousand taste buds that are sensitive to chemical compounds. The greatest number of them are on the tip and sides of the tongue, so that the tongue is more important for taste sensations than the palate and mouth cavity. But the number of taste buds varies from person to person. Some people have only a hundred, some easily four hundred per square centimeter—depending on their genes. Super-tasters with four hundred taste buds react strongly to sharp spices, for example, while people with only one hundred can be considered practically non-tasters. At least their perception threshold is greatly reduced. Super-tasters and non-tasters each account for about 25 percent of the population, while the other 50 percent are considered normal-tasters. Also, the ability to taste declines steadily as you grow older. At the age of eighty, a person has only about a third of the active taste buds he or she had at twenty. Moreover, the tongue can register only four tastes: sweet, sour, salt, and bitter. It is incapable of finer distinctions. The centers for the perception of these separate tastes lie in different parts of the tongue where taste buds are concentrated.

The Nose

The nose, more precisely the mucous membrane, is a far more sensitive organ than the tongue. It contains some 1.5 million sensory cells capable of distinguishing a broad spectrum of scents. Most of what people think they are tasting they are actually smelling. The level at which scents are perceived differs from person to person. The sense of smell also declines with age. In contrast to

The nose is a far more sensitive organ than the tongue: a person actually smells most of what he thinks he is tasting.

taste, however, the sense of smell can be trained. This means that even older wine-drinkers can develop a "super-nose," while untrained young people can be true "non-smellers" when it comes to wine. If a person "tastes" better with the nose than the tongue, it is logical to wonder why wine drinkers taste wines at all. The answer is simple: Taste buds not only taste but "feel" a wine. They are connected to the trigeminal nerve, by which tactile sensations in the mouth are delivered to the brain. Thus, the tongue perceives the wine's viscosity, its velvetiness (or roughness), and its temperature.

SMELLING AND TASTING

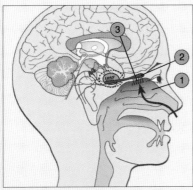

Smell: Scent molecules pass through (1) the nose to (2) the olfactory bulb. (3) By way of its cilia (tiny hairs), the chemical stimulus is transformed into an electric signal.

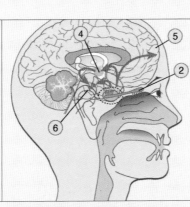

Scent Perception: On the way from (2) the olfactory bulb to the cerebrum the scent stimulus first passes (4) the hypothalamus, which produces sensations of pleasure and aversion. Only then is the smell consciously experienced in (5) the cortex. The memory of the scent is stored in (6) the hippocampus.

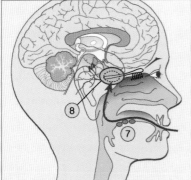

Taste Stimulus: The wine on the tongue stimulates (7) the taste buds, which are connected to (8) the taste center (gyrus hippocampi) in the cortex. Along the way, the taste is experienced as pleasant or unpleasant. At the same time, the wine is "felt" by way of the trigeminal nerve.

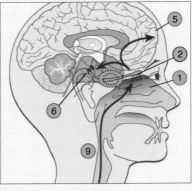

Retronasal smelling: After the wine has been swallowed, its scent again rises up in (9) the throat and reaches (1) the nasal cavity. By way of (2) the olfactory bulb, the scent stimulus is again passed to (5) the cortex, compared with the stored recollection of the scent (6), identified, and thus reexperienced.

TIPS & TRICKS

A simple test lets you determine whether you are among non-tasters or normal-tasters. Blindfolded, first taste a teaspoon of fresh milk then a teaspoon of cream. If the taste buds cannot distinguish the differing viscosity of the two fatty substances you are a non-taster, one who likewise perceives other distinctions in taste to a lesser degree than other tasters.

WHAT THE TONGUE TASTES

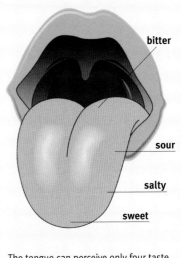

bitter

sour

salty

sweet

The tongue can perceive only four taste sensations; more refined distinctions are beyond its ability.

How a Wine Ought to Taste

Every grape variety has its own typical aromas. With white wines, which are usually made from a single variety, experienced wine drinkers can recognize the variety relatively easily. Recognition is more difficult with red wines, as they are frequently made from several different varieties of grapes.

White Wines

Wines made from only a single variety should have the "pure" taste of that variety. Especially in white wines, typicity is a criterion of quality. But *terroir*—the combined effect of slope, soil, and climate on grapes—also greatly influences a wine.

The aroma typical of a given variety differs from one growing region to another. Many white wines made from the same variety bear only a remote resemblance— Chablis and Pouilly Fuissé for example. Both are produced from Chardonnay grapes that are grown in soils composed of chalk and clay; but one thrives in the

north of Burgundy, the other in the south. As a result, Chablis develops aromas like citron and grapefruit, Pouilly Fuissé those of nuts, almonds, and honey.

WHITE WINE AROMAS

Chardonnay	Hazelnut, honeydew melon, citron, grapefruit, banana
Chasselas	Green apples, daisies
Chenin Blanc	Apples, hazelnuts, mandarin oranges
Cortese	Apples, lemon blossoms
Fiano	Quince, pineapple, mandarin oranges, honey, hazelnuts
Gewürztraminer	Tea roses, litchi, figs, quince
Grüner Veltliner	Peppers, pea-pods, pepper
Muscadet	Grapefruit, lemon peel, anise
Neuburger	Apples, hazelnuts
Pinot Blanc	Pears, quince jam, tea
Pinot Gris	Potatoes, bread, roasted hazelnuts, bacon
Prosecco	Litchi, lemon blossoms
Riesling	Peaches, apricots, honeydew melon, petrol
Sauvignon Blanc	Peppers, green tomatoes, black currants, gooseberries
Sémillon	Peaches, pineapple, honey, saffron
Silvaner	Apples, potatoes, fennel, celery
Tokai	Apples, linden blossoms
Trebbiano	Apples, fresh bread
Verdicchio	Quince, pears, hay, orange peel
Vermentino	Apples, lemon balm, fresh hay
Viognier	Apricots, pears, lemon grass, almonds, honey
Welshriesling	Apples, acacia blossoms

PALLISER E

MARTINBOROU
CHARDONNA
1995

Produced and bottled by Palliser E
Kitchener Street, Martinboro

Red Wines

With red wines, the aroma typical of the variety varies even more. A Chilean Cabernet Sauvignon presents, in addition to the currant note typical of all the world's Cabernets, a tone reminiscent of mint or eucalyptus candies. Experienced wine drinkers can identify Chilean Cabernets blindfolded, due to this note. A Cabernet from Bordeaux never presents eucalyptus, but rather a cedar note. Moreover, some red wines are made from several different grape varieties, so aromas are blended more than in white wines. Not only are *terroir* distinctions recognizable in all types of wines, but the influence of the cellar master is sometimes more evident in reds than whites. For example, cellar masters must decide how long to leave red wines in contact with grape skins, but they don't have to decide this for most white wines, which in general are left in contact with grape skins only briefly, if at all.

RED WINE AROMAS

Aglianico	Plums, violets, venison
Barbera	Sour cherries, cloves, marmalade, tobacco
Blauer zeigelt	Cherry juice, elderberries, cloves
Blaufränkish	Blackberries, cherry jam, musk, bitter chocolate
Cabernet Franc	Blueberries, green pepper, peppers, grass
Cabernet Sauvignon	Currants, cedar wood, black pepper, cloves, eucalyptus
Carignane	Fruit compote, blueberries, laurel, rosemary
Gamay	Raspberry drops, bananas, cloves
Grenache	Blackberry jam, raisins, tobacco
Malbec	Sour cherries, cooked plums, pepper, cinnamon
Merlot	Blackberries, currants, baked plums, truffles
Mourvèdre	Fruit compote, leather, game
Nebbiolo	Cherry jam, cinnamon, dried flowers, tar
Pinot Noir	Raspberries, cherry marmalade, plums, cloves
Pinotage	Sour cherries, plums, bananas, pepper, cinnamon
Sangiovese	Blackberries, cranberries, green wood, leather, vanilla
Syrah (Shiraz)	Black currants, truffles, dried meat, violets
Tannat	Mulberries, blueberries, cedar wood, pepper, dried meat
Tempranillo	Blackberries, cranberries, currants, sandalwood, musk
Zinfandel	Black currants, cooked plums, bananas, pepper

Wine and Health

The French cardinal Armand Jean du Plessis Richelieu was fond of tweaking his clerical colleagues with the admonition, "If God forbade drinking, why does he make such good wines grow?" As a man of God, he was obliged to censure the rampant drunkenness of the time, yet as a man of the absolutist era, he knew how to value physical pleasures. That these, so far as wine is concerned, were no threat to his health, he knew better than many laymen today.

Hangovers and Headaches

Many people do not even notice that their bodies metabolize alcohol more slowly than they consume it. To fully metabolize a single glass of wine takes the body about an hour. More alcohol can have unpleasant consequences: headache and an upset stomach serve as warnings that the wine drinker has stepped beyond his limit.

For headache there is only one effective remedy: acetylsalicylic acid. More commonly known as aspirin, it is a component in many headache pills.

The Hangover

Everyone knows the feeling: first giddiness and dizziness, then a throbbing headache, finally vomiting and moral contrition—revenge for overindulgence in alcohol the night before. A hangover after generous indulgence in wine is no less unpleasant just because it is due to a culturally respected drink. Those who suffer from it only wish it to end as soon as possible. But the hangover does have its good side: it lets the wine drinker know how much alcohol he can tolerate.

One Glass an Hour

A good 90 percent of the alcohol a person consumes is metabolized in the liver, which produces an enzyme called ADH (aldehyde dehydrogenase) that breaks down alcohol first into toxic acetaldehyde, then into acetic acid. This is metabolized by the body and eliminated through the intestine. An average liver breaks down roughly 8 to 10 grams of alcohol an hour—roughly the amount in a glass of wine. If a person drinks more than this within an hour, the excess cannot be immediately processed by the liver. The alcohol or acetaldehyde enters the bloodstream and is carried to the parts of the body that are rich in blood vessels, such as the brain. The results are dizziness and grogginess.

Acetaldehyde

Headaches are caused by increased liquid pressure in the brain. Acetaldehyde does not only circulate in the blood but travels throughout the body; you can even smell a high concentration of acetaldehyde on a person's breath and skin. Because it readily dissolves in water, it penetrates directly into the tissues, expanding the tissue cells so that they release water—roughly like a sponge under pressure.

This causes perspiration, and results in dehydration that is also noticeable internally, especially in the brain. Since the water released there cannot escape, it creates excessive pressure that is perceived as a headache.

Men and Women

Men produce significantly more ADH than women, and thus can metabolize alcohol faster. For this reason, women tolerate alcohol less as a rule, though there are exceptions. In addition to ADH, another enzyme—MEOS (microsomal ethanol oxidizing system)—can break down alcohol. Normally MEOS processes only 5 percent of the alcohol consumed, but with frequent alcohol consumption this system (in contrast to ADH) becomes more effective, processing up to 30 percent. Even so, it is still true that two glasses of wine in an hour overtax the body, whether male or female. Sparkling wine and wine spritzers release alcohol into the blood even more quickly, as do sweet wines. Wine drinkers should therefore be especially wary of sparkling or liqueur wines.

Sulfur and Histamines

Excessive consumption of alcohol is by far the chief cause of headaches after drinking wine, but not the only one. In sensitive people a wine high in sulfur (which is added to nearly all wines on the market, to prevent premature oxidation) can cause headache, though the percentage of people who react to sulfur in this way is quite small. Sulfur is more likely to lead to stomach pains, as the compounds it forms with other substances in wine can break down into their original components in the acidic conditions of the stomach.

Histamines, protein components that are undesirable byproducts of the biological breakdown of acid in many chardonnays and all red wines, can also result in headaches by causing the dilation of capillaries, in the same way that skin reacts to an insect bite by swelling. This happens only rarely, but when it does, even small amounts of wine (5 to 8 milligrams) are enough to provoke a reaction.

TIPS AND TRICKS: FIGHTING HEADACHE

For headache and hangover there is only one miracle drug: acetylsalicylic acid, the most common component of headache pills. You can therefore prevent a hangover if you take one or two tablets—in which the primary ingredient is aspirin—before going to bed. If these are taken in an effervescent form, they will be absorbed even faster. Vitamins C and E assist the liver in metabolizing the alcohol, but once the hangover has begun, it is generally too late for pills: the stomach can no longer process them. Smoking while drinking will make matters worse, since nicotine heightens the effect of alcohol. Drinking water—contrary to popular belief—only hastens the spread of alcohol through the body.

Stomach Comfort

In some people, white wines regularly produce heartburn and stomachache. Others react to red wine with a rapid heartbeat. Often it is only specific red or wine wines that produce such reactions—sometimes after just one glass.

Wine in the Stomach

The last stop for the alcohol consumed—at least temporarily—is the stomach. The minute it arrives there, it stimulates the production of gastric acid, which breaks down fat and protein and makes digestion possible. For this reason wine is commonly consumed with meals in many cultures. Gastric acid, which is made up of pepsin and hydrochloric acid, ensures that the stomach has a pH value less than 1: that is, quite acid. In people who produce a lot of gastric acid, the consumption of large quantities of alcohol can therefore lead to irritation of the stomach's mucous membranes and the duodenum. White wines especially, which have higher levels of acid (pH 2.8 to 3), can cause stomachache, heartburn, and inflammation of the stomach membranes. Too rapid ingestion of alcohol can be problematic even in people who are not overly sensitive, hindering the activity of the hormones that stimulate gastric acid production, and thus creating an alkaline environment. Any food consumed at the same time remains undigested. The result: bloating and lassitude.

Pickled herring as a hangover breakfast can restore the acid balance in the stomach.

The Nervous System

Alcohol itself is absorbed by the stomach and transported to the liver. On an empty stomach, the alcohol in a glass of wine takes only forty minutes to reach the liver, where it is processed—first oxidized to acetaldehyde and then changed into acetate (acetic acid), which is then slowly metabolized in tissues and musculature. This becomes problematic if you drink too quickly, for the liver is then flooded with large quantities of alcohol that it cannot handle. Alcohol and acetaldehyde remain in the blood. Since both substances are water soluble, they penetrate from the blood into surrounding tissues and attack the central nervous system. The first symptoms of excessive alcohol consumption are reduced perception, dizziness, and loss of balance. The alcohol expands blood vessels, leading to increased dehydration through perspiration and urination.

Nausea

Allergies to wine or specific substances in wine are extremely rare. Rashes or asthma are most uncommon, and vomiting is never an allergic reaction but simply a consequence of overindulgence, one of the typical symptoms of a hangover. With repeated vomiting the stomach is emptied not only of solid nourishment but also of all its gastric acid. After recovery, it is therefore soothing to reintroduce acid into the stomach. This is why people recommend a hangover breakfast of pickled herring or sour pickles. The speed with which the body processes the alcohol depends on several factors, among them the contents of the stomach. Fatty and protein-rich foods slow alcohol absorption. Cheese and milk counter the effect of alcohol most effectively, and spicy foods also slow its passage through the stomach and the wall of the intestine. The alcohol from a glass of wine taken can take an hour or two to enter the bloodstream on a full stomach, but only about forty minutes on an empty one.

Calories

Wine is highly caloric, with the majority of its calories deriving from alcohol. A 25-fluid ounce bottle of wine contains on an average 500 calories. Regular wine consumption can therefore make you gain weight, but this is not automatic: in people of average or less than average weight, alcohol does not necessarily contribute to weight gain. People who are already overweight, however, can put on additional pounds as the result of drinking wine. The acetaldehyde slows the breakdown of fat in the tissues. This is true of alcohol in general, not only wine. In addition, wine stimulates the appetite, leading people to consume greater amounts of food. All in all, the effect of alcohol on a person's weight is dependent on his or her specific metabolism.

TIPS AND TRICKS: NAUSEA

It is necessary to compensate for the body's loss of water and salt by drinking large quantities of liquids, but teas or warm soups are better than ordinary tap water or mineral water. Sweets also help restore the sugar content in the blood. It is not surprising that Coca-Cola and salted pretzels are commonly consumed as a means of hastening recovery after nausea and vomiting. A bite of raw ginger can stop the retching and calm the stomach. Easing headache and nausea with an additional glass of wine may work, but this is dangerous—fighting alcohol with alcohol is the first step to addiction.

CALORIES FROM ALCOHOL

8% per volume	325 cal / 87 cal
9% per volume	366 cal / 98 cal
10% per volume	413 cal / 110 cal
11% per volume	450 cal / 120 cal
12% per volume	498 cal / 133 cal
13% per volume	535 cal / 143 cal
14% per volume	578 cal / 154 cal
15% per volume	620 cal / 165 cal

(Number of calories in a 25-fluid ounce bottle or 6.8-fluid ounce glass of wine, depending on alcohol content.)

Wine and the Heart

People have always felt ambivalent about wine. While some have celebrated it as a drink for connoisseurs, others have fought it as a drug. Until quite recently the positive effects of wine consumption have been generally ignored, but in 1991 the "French paradox," which seems to indicate that moderate wine consumption is healthier than abstinence, became a popular subject of debate.

Moderate Consumption

On November 17, 1991, CBS began broadcasting a new series of its regular discussion program *60 Minutes* on the subject of healthy diets. The moderator, Morley Safer, lifted a glass of red wine, declaring that it was possible that the reason for France's low rate of heart attacks was contained in this glass. The discussion that followed electrified viewers and occupied Americans for years. Most of all, it completely overturned our previous thinking about wine. Suddenly this dangerous drug was being hailed as a preventative against America's number-one killer: heart attack resulting from the fatty degeneration of the coronary arteries. The controversy also captivated the European public and mobilized scientists, wine lobbyists, and health officials. What people in winegrowing regions already knew from their own experience was suddenly official: moderate wine consumption is part of a healthy lifestyle. This is especially true of red wine.

Fewer Heart Attacks

Where did CBS get its information? It compared the results of studies of the "unhealthy" lifestyle of French males with similar studies carried out in America. Frenchmen, these studies revealed, smoke considerably more than their American counterparts. They get less exercise and consume roughly 30 percent more fat in the form of butter, cheese, ham, and foie gras. Moreover, the French tend to drink red wine even at lunchtime. Per capita consumption of red wine in France is ten times that of America. Yet French men suffer from 30 to 50 percent fewer heart attacks. This paradox led scientists to the conclusion that the red wine compensates for an otherwise unhealthy lifestyle. Red wine, they suspected, somehow protects the coronary arteries, and can therefore guard against heart attack.

Wine and Cholesterol

Since then, these suspicions have been confirmed. In fact, three substances in red wine have an antioxidant effect: the phenols quercetin, catechin, and above all resveratrol. Phenols are found in all wines, but they are ten times more abundant in red than in white wines. The more tannin-rich the wine, the greater the quantity of phenols. In other words, it is tannin (or tannic acid) that protects the heart, raising the production of HDL (high-density lipoprotein) while reducing that of dangerous, cholesterol-rich LDL (low-density lipoprotein). In people who consume large quantities of fat, LDL collects on the walls of the coronary arteries, constricting them and possibly triggering heart attack. Moreover, it bonds with oxygen and draws it out of the bloodstream, so that the heart muscle is under-supplied. Red wine, with its high tannin content, prevents this: the tannin oxidizes the cholesterol and ensures that it is metabolized.

WINE ALONE IS NOT ENOUGH

It is unlikely that people anywhere drink wine only to protect themselves from heart attack. Wine is an intoxicant, and is treated as such: those who wish to protect themselves against heart attack would do better to switch to a low-fat, low-cholesterol diet, get enough exercise, and take supplementary vitamin E and beta-carotene, known to be effective coronary preventatives thanks to their antioxidant properties. However, knowing about wine's health benefits can certainly help you enjoy it without guilt.

Red Wine, A Unique Beverage

The French paradox does not apply to hard liquor, beer, or other alcoholic drinks—only to red wine, and then only when it is drunk in moderation. Moderate wine consumption means enjoyment within limits. To put it another way, you should take advantage of wine's positive qualities without succumbing to its negative ones. It would be a mistake to begin drinking as much red wine as possible to maximize the beneficial effects of its tannin. The wine may be good for your heart, but the alcohol it contains can damage your liver, stomach, intestines, and nervous system if consumed in excessive quantity.

Daily Wine Intake

The experts don't necessarily agree about what "moderation" means. It used to be that agricultural laborers allowed themselves a bottle a day of ordinary wine, or half a bottle of a wine with a higher alcohol content. But back then ordinary wine was so thin that it could not even be sold under today's regulations, and it was often further weakened with water. Nowadays doctors feel that one or two glasses a day (.1 liter each) are acceptable for women, three glasses for men. These recommendations are made in an effort to avoid any possible risk. If consumers were to take the doctors at their word, two people could never order a bottle of wine—unless they were pre-

pared to leave a fourth of it untouched. However, experience shows that two healthy people who are neither underweight nor diabetic can regularly empty a bottle without doing damage to their livers. Nevertheless, the wine's alcohol content needs to be taken into consideration. A German Riesling with a slight residual sweetness contains about 9 percent alcohol by volume, while a heavy Californian chardonnay or an Italian Barolo, by contrast, can have 14 percent—more than half again as much. For people who do no physical work and get little exercise, that can be too much.

Many doctors, scientists, and politicians will need to revise their idea of a healthy lifestyle. Drinking a little wine is healthier than abstinence—such is the lesson of the "French paradox". This goes particularly for red wine with high tannin levels.

Wine Accessories

Wine alone is not enough. The right accessories are also a part of it. "We were forced to drink water all day because he had no corkscrew," complained the writer Robert Louis Stevenson after a meeting with his publisher.

Equipment for the Beginner

People who have only one set of wineglasses in their cupboard enjoy the advantage of not having to think twice about which glass to choose. There are many all-purpose glasses that will do even for high-quality wines. Once you have the basic equipment you can concentrate on what is essential: the wine. But as you gain more experience with wine, you may want to keep on hand different glasses for different wines, provided you have the space. But then, of course, choosing the right wine for the occasion becomes more difficult.

Basic Equipment

All-purpose glass (either with long stem, tall bowl, or standard dimensions) for white wine, red wine, and sparkling wine
Waiter's friend

Glasses: Riedel, Nachtmann, Ikea; waiter's friend: Screwpull "Sharky"

More Ambitious Basic Equipment

White-wine glass
Red-wine glass
Sparkling-wine glass
Corkscrew
Bottle cooler

Glasses: Schott Zwiesel "Diva"; corkscrew: Screwpull "Elite"; cooler: Screwpull "Wine Cooler"

Equipment for the Most Demanding

Every wine drinker has his own expectations. But the number of people who stick to only a single wine is clearly declining. Most wine lovers have become more adventuresome, one day fetching a light Italian Gavi from their cooler, the next day opening an old Spanish Rioja, looking forward to the next sweet Beerenauslese from Germany, and on the weekend indulging in a Champagne on the terrace. Anyone who is so well-supplied with wine needs a few useful accessories, most of all suitable glasses.

Most Advanced Equipment

White wine goblet
Young white wine glass
Champagne flute
Red wine goblet
Red wine glass magnum
Decanting carafe (not shown)
Ice bucket
Capsule cutter
High-tech corkscrew
Champagne pliers
Pouring spout
Wine thermometer

Glasses: Spiegelau "Vino Grande"; corkscrew: VacuVin Winemaster;
Champagne pliers; wine thermometer: Exquisit; Champagne stopper:
Screwpull "Crown"; pouring foil: "Drop Stop"; ice bucket:
Firmenpräsent Billecart-Salmon

Equipment for Professionals

Those who not only drink wines but also collect them deny themselves nothing when it comes to accessories. If expense is no object, such people ought to build their houses around the wine cellar, making sure to plan for glass cupboards large enough to hold an array of glasses, carafes, and other accessories. Most wine collectors do not keep their prizes solely to themselves. When they invite friends to a rare-bottle party, a single glass simply will not do.

Glassware: Riedel; corkscrew, standing model: Screwpull "Leverpull"; butler's friend: "Monopol"

Ultimate Equipment

Riesling glass
White wine glass for Chardonnay
White wine glass for Montrachet
Sekt glass
Vintage Champagne glass
Sweet wine glass for Sauternes
Red wine glass for a Hermitage
Red wine glass for aged Bordeaux
Red wine glass for Burgundy *grand cru*
Vintage Port glass
Carafe for a single bottle
Carafe for a magnum
High-tech corkscrew
Butler's friend
Ice-cube glass
Silver Champagne bowl for 5 bottles
Decanting funnel

Champagne bowl: HCH; decanting funnel: Provino; bottle thermometer and aroma stopper: Screwpull

Storing and Buying Wine

Wine is most comfortable at cool temperatures, say, that of London in a November fog. But the humidity should be that of a beach in the Caribbean. At the same time, it wants to be in a space that is as dark and still as a tomb. Only then is it assured of a long life. Such conditions must be artificially created.

Temperature and Humidity

Few wines have the potential to age for fifty years or more. Such bottles are considered precious and are sold at top prices. That they were able to reach that age is thanks to a fine vintage, the genius of the cellar master, and a proper cellar.

Two great old wines that have only now reached their full development: a 1964 Erbacher Marcobrunn Riesling Cabinet Auslese and a 1947 Château Cheval Blanc.

Robust Everyday Wines

Everyday wines are robust because in their production nothing is left to chance. They are created "by the book": refined, stabilized, filtered, and provided with a precisely measured dose of sulfur appropriate to their predicted life span. Sanitation during production is also taken more seriously than it once was. Undesirable germs and bacteria are eliminated at an early stage, and bottles and corks rigorously sterilized. In this respect, everyday wines, at least, are not unlike industrial products—a boon for the consumer. They not only survive long drives in the car without damage but even shipment halfway around the world. They weather brief fluctuations in temperature with aplomb. They are stable in heat and relatively resistant to cold. Even violent vibrations do not put them permanently out of balance. In short, most wines are more durable than alarmist journalists would have wine drinkers believe.

Sensitive Top-Quality Wines

But their durability is not without limits. Unfavorable storage conditions have a negative influence on the development of a wine over the long term. This is especially true of expensive, high-quality wines. As a rule, they are not "prepared" as well as simple everyday wines. Exacting wine producers strive to treat the grapes, the must, and the wine in their cellars as gently as possible so as to preserve aroma, taste, and natural harmoniousness. Fine wines are generally only minimally refined, frequently not filtered at all, and almost always under-sulfured. Overly-warm storage, excessive light, or frequent motion can do considerable damage to them. Those who buy wines that are meant to age more than two or three years must therefore understand the conditions for proper storage.

Temperature and Humidity

The optimal cellar temperature is a constant one. It should be between 42°F (6°C) and 62°F (16°C). Even 68°F (20°C) will not harm the wine, though the alcohol will evaporate more rapidly at higher temperatures. Moreover, in wines that have not been perfectly stabilized, too much warmth can encourage a secondary fermentation, which may cause the cork to be forced out of the bottle. Just as important as temperature is humidity. The ideal is 75 percent. At less than 60 percent the cellar is too dry. Corks may shrivel, seals may break, and bottles may begin to leak or exhibit greater ullage due to the increased evaporation. To be sure, this only happens after three or more years of storage. At more than 85% humidity labels may stain, corks may turn moldy, and the cellar may take on a musty smell.

Cellars in Old Buildings

Those who own cellars in old buildings are fortunate indeed. They are generally dark and naturally cool. Since the outside walls are probably not insulated, the humidity is generally higher than in the cellars of new buildings, minimalizing the change in ullage. Almost ideal conditions for wine—as long as there are no heating ducts running across the walls. The only problems are deviations in temperature, which can be substantial in uninsulated buildings. Between summer and winter the temperature may vary by 50°F (10°C) and more, which is too much. Even so, it is possible to block up and insulate cellar windows, and nearby heating ducts can be wrapped in thick foam sleeves so that they do not radiate heat. If none of these measures helps, it may be necessary to install a cooling system. Otherwise, the wine may suffer damage over the long term.

TIPS & TRICKS: STORE BOTTLES UPRIGHT

According to custom, wine bottles are generally stored horizontally to keep their corks moist. But simple everyday wines can be stored upright with no problem. The cork will not dry out over a period of only a few months, and the risk of "corkiness" is low. But vertical storage has advantages even with wines capable of aging. The wine's surface area exposed to oxygen is less in the vertical than in the horizontal position, so it may age more slowly and stay fresh longer. When storing bottles vertically, high humidity is required (about 80 percent) so that corks do not dry out.

Coolers and Climate Chests

Where cellars are too warm and living rooms too dry, there is no place for wines that are meant to age except a climate chest. These are even better and safer than a cool cellar.

New-Building Cellars

Cellars in new buildings are often warmer than living rooms. The heating ducts and hot-water pipes running across the ceiling make for temperatures of more than 68°F (20°C) during the winter heating months, and the air is correspondingly dry. Such cellars are therefore unsuitable for storing wine—whether in a separate room or an alcove. The best solution is to install a cooler or wine climate-chest, or to construct a cool cell.

Cooler

A bottle cooler is useful for keeping 20 to 50 bottles chilled for a short time. It works on the principle of a regular refrigerator: When the thermostat registers that the temperature has fallen 5 degrees, the device switches on and restores the former temperature. Constantly fluctuating temperatures mean that the wine alternately expands and contracts. Coolers are therefore unsuitable for longer storage. Moreover, coolers are too dry. The humidity collects on the cooling plates as ice and is later defrosted.

Wine Climate Chest

A climate chest is suitable even for long-term storage. Humidity drawn out of the air is replaced, and they are vibration-free. The temperature, despite variations in the outside temperature, remains virtually constant (+/−2 degrees). In addition bottles can be stored in different climate zones: noble red wines on the top shelf at 66°F (18°C), Champagnes on the bottom one at 42°F (6°C). In some models it is possible to store original wooden cases. Depending on size and maker, wine climate chests accommodate from 40 to 1,000 bottles. There is only one thing they cannot do: guarantee that after ten years the bottles will not be covered with dust and cobwebs.

Many wine producers bottle a portion of their wines in magnums, which not only have show value but also aging benefits.

*Used almost exclusively for Champagnes

*Nebuchadnezzar	*Balthazar	*Salmanasar	Impériale	Jeroboam	Double magnum	Magnum	Normal bottle
15 l	12 l	9 l	6 l	5 l	3 l	1.5 l	0.75 l
(16 quarts)	(12.5 quarts)	(9.5 quarts)	(6.25 quarts)	(5.25 quarts)	(3 quarts)	(1.5 quarts)	(0.75 quarts)

Cooler: For longer storage, a refrigerator is unsuitable because of temperature variations and possible odors. But it does a fine job of chilling.

Combined thermometer and hygrometer: Part of the basic equipment of every wine cellar. In this example, the top gauge records temperature, and the bottom, humidity.

Thermometer: Cellars in old buildings are subject to deviations in temperature. A thermometer is a necessary instrument for registering them.

Wine Climate Chest: The interior is divided into different climate zones. The top stays at 66°F (18°C) for red wines, the bottom at 46°F (8°C) for white wines. Humidity can be regulated.

CHECK LIST FOR STORAGE

Storage units: Metal and wooden shelves are especially space-saving; pumice-stone blocks help regulate humidity.

Smells: Damp cellars with musty smells need to be regularly aired. Otherwise the wine picks up odors. Kitchens, garages, and cellar rooms with oil tanks are taboo for storing wine.

Light: Direct sunlight soon causes red wines to turn pale and white wines to become a golden yellow. The quality of Champagne suffers from even the least amount of light. Solution: Darken the space or keep valuable wines in cases or other packaging.

Noise: Regular noises from heating units and cooling devices damage wine in the long run. Insulate windows and put soundproof material on the ceiling.

Vibrations: Shaking from passing truck and train traffic prevents age-worthy wines from ever coming to rest. Solution: Place shelving on rubber or cork pads.

Dampness: In cellars that are too dry, it is necessary to use a humidifier. Two buckets of water can serve the same purpose. Cellars that are too damp should get a layer of sand or gravel on the floor.

Wine cartons: Cardboard absorbs dampness. Cartons are not suitable for long storage in dry cellars.

Mildewed labels: An indication of well-humidified air. The wine does not suffer at all, though its resale value is adversely affected.

Peeling labels: An indication that a cellar is too dry.

Rented space: In the United States, the practice of renting secure wine-cellar space with ideal storage conditions is widespread. Such services are becoming increasingly available in large European cities as well.

Storing Wine in an Apartment

Storing wine in a three-room apartment requires ingenuity. Look in the coldest room in the apartment for niches where wooden cases, cartons, or wooden shelving can be accommodated. Such corners can become wine stashes for a few months, or even years if necessary.

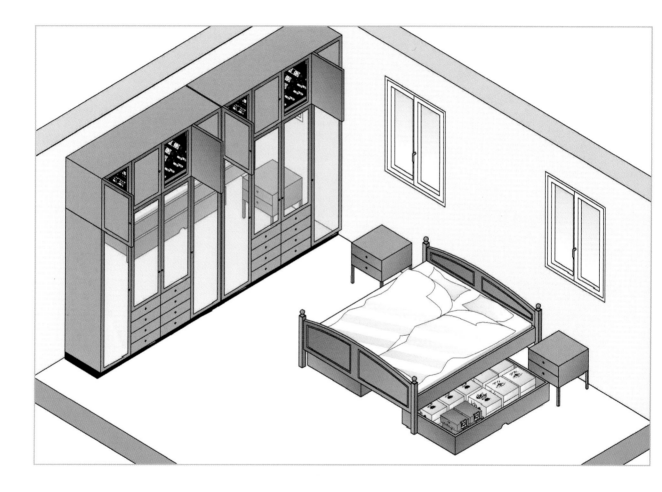

Wine in the Bedroom

The coolest room in an apartment can be the bedroom if it is on the north side of the building or faces north, because it does not become too warm in summer. In winter the heat can be turned off, as heat entering from the other rooms is adequate. This means that the bedroom is often three or four degrees cooler than south-facing rooms—not ideal for wine storage but still better than the kitchen or the garage. If you are able to keep the room temperature at roughly 46°F (8°C), wines can be stored there for a few years with no problem. The top shelves of a wardrobe are one possible spot for wine cases and cartons—provided that the room is not used for drying laundry. You can also place shelving above a wardrobe; depending on the height involved, it may be possible to accommodate up to 250 bottles between it and the ceiling. To get at the wine, simply use a step ladder. Another possible place is the unused space under the bed, which could also possibly take 100 or 150 bottles. Just remember to air the room regularly.

Wine in the Kitchen

Every apartment has corners or angles in which spaces can be easily walled off for storing wine. Such a space need only be large enough to hold a couple of shelving units and a small cooling device that will ensure a favorable temperature. The dividing walls can be made of ordinary particleboard; it is only necessary that it be protected against warmth, odors, and noise with three layers of polyester. With such protection, a storage closet can even be installed in a kitchen, the warmest room in an apartment and the one with the most odors. In the United States, there are complete kits available, costing anywhere from $200 to $500, depending on size. But it is easy enough to put one together yourself. With a little skill and the right tools you can create your own wine "cellar."

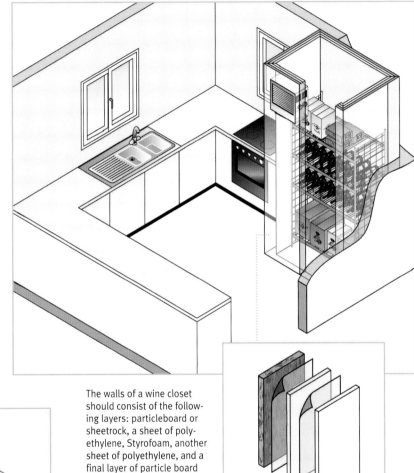

The walls of a wine closet should consist of the following layers: particleboard or sheetrock, a sheet of polyethylene, Styrofoam, another sheet of polyethylene, and a final layer of particle board or sheetrock.

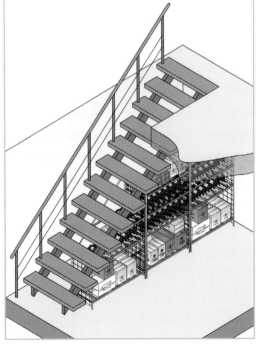

Wine under the Stairs

In duplex apartments, the space under the stairs is often unused. Without great expense, it is possible to set up custom-built shelving there that will easily have room for 100 to 150 bottles. If you wish, you can seal off the storage area with wood. A cooling unit is not recommended because of the noise. In any case, stairwells, foyers, and corridors are generally cooler than living rooms.

Outfitting a Wine Cellar

The notion of storing wine underground dates from a time when cellars were naturally cool.
In the age of the modern apartment building, cellar spaces are nearly as warm as living spaces.
The central heating unit and hot-water pipes emit more heat than cellar owners might wish.
It is therefore necessary to create a consistently cool cellar-climate artificially.

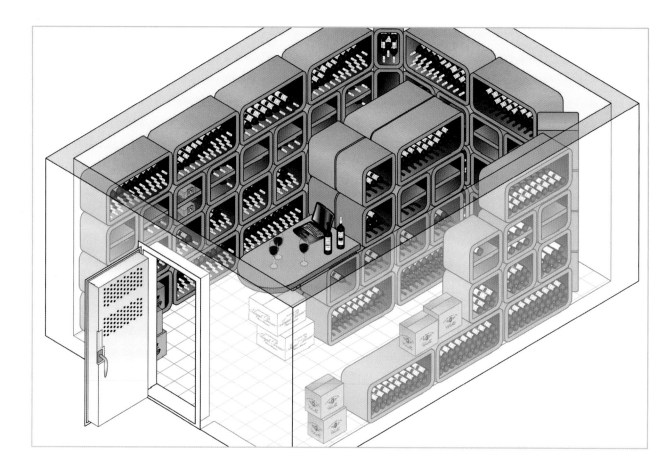

Cellar with Climate Door

A perfectly climatized storeroom for more than 2,000 bottles can be made out of an ordinary cellar room of 59 feet (18 square meters). First the cellar window needs to be walled up. Then any heating ducts running across the ceiling need to be insulated. Thick foam sleeves are easily installed and absorb 99 percent of the radiation. Then you need to install a special, thick-walled climate door. It contains a cooling device, regulated by a microprocessor, that blows cool air into the cellar space. The best of these doors can climatize spaces of up to 52 cubic yards (40 cubic meters). That means 59 feet (18 square meters) with a ceiling height of 7 and a quarter feet (2.20 meters). You can select any room temperature between 43°F (6°C) and 68°F (20°C). If the outside temperature drops drastically in winter the cellar room may also be heated. In addition to its climate function, the door regulates the humidity (from 60 to 80 percent is standard). An active charcoal filter also purifies the air.

Cellar with Climate Closet

Many people who live in rental apartments have only a fenced off storage space in the cellar instead of a separate room. In this situation, it is impossible to insulate the walls and heating pipes. But there is nothing to prevent you from creating a climate-controlled wine closet in such a space. Even with a floor area of only 18 square feet (2 square meters) you will be able to store up to 500 bottles. There are various technical standards for such a climate-controlled cell, depending on the manufacturer. The simplest versions have only air-conditioning. Between its cooling and resting phases, inside temperatures will vary by roughly 5°F (-15°C). Climate-controlled cells can be put together in your basement and dismantled again if you move.

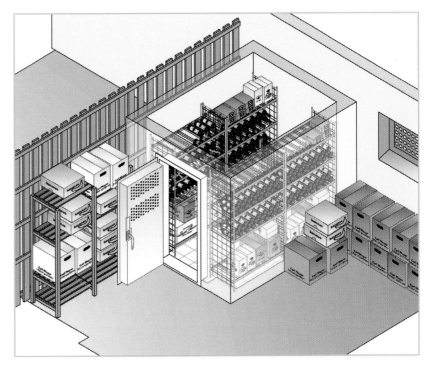

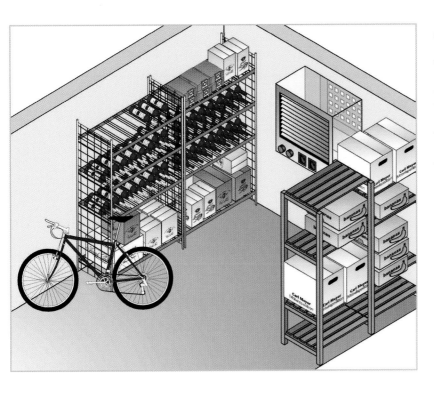

Cellar with Air-Conditioning

Small, closed-off cellar spaces can be cooled with air-conditioning just like a living room. The cooler can be installed in the cellar window. Installation is uncomplicated, the energy used is minimal, and the cost of the machine is low. But be sure that the noise does not disturb other residents or neighbors. Wines that are meant to age only two or three years can easily survive the small variations in temperature that occur with this minimal solution.

Cellar Management with Computer Software

Today you can keep track of your inventory on a computer. With the appropriate software, you can register considerably more than simple additions and subtractions.

The Cellar Log

To be sure, it is possible to drink wine without keeping notes. It is also possible to buy wines, store them, and serve them without a cellar log. But if you are a wine professional, there is no way that you can avoid keeping records. A conscientiously kept register can also be helpful if you buy wines only as a hobby. For example, if you decide to buy wines that need to age a few years before they can be truly enjoyed, it is well worth documenting them, as it is if you are fortunate enough to own hundreds or thousands of bottles. Moreover, keeping a cellar log is quite simple: you need only enter what you purchase and on the same page record your consumption of it along with comments. In this way you always have an overview of your holdings, the number of bottles, and the progress of specific vintages. A cellar log requires only a few facts: the purchase date, the name and vintage of the wine, the source, the price, and the quantity. Below this record the date on which you removed the wine, the number of bottles remaining, and possibly the occasion for drinking it, the dish it accompanied, and your personal impressions.

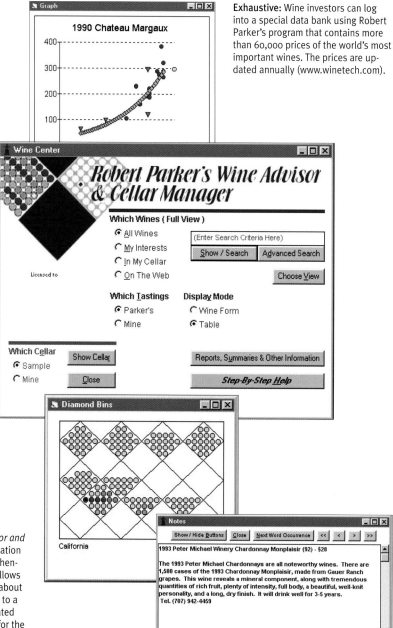

Exhaustive: Wine investors can log into a special data bank using Robert Parker's program that contains more than 60,000 prices of the world's most important wines. The prices are updated annually (www.winetech.com).

Exemplary: With *Robert Parker's Wine Advisor and Cellar Manager* you can enter the precise location of a given wine in your cellar and call it up whenever you wish. A link to the *Wine Advocate* allows you to access information and review notes about 34,000 wines, and wine investors can log on to a special database (www.winetech.com), updated annually, that lists more than 60,000 prices for the world's most important wines.

Computer Software

A wide range of software is available to help you manage your wine cellar. Simple programs merely keep track of inventory, as in the traditional cellar log. More elaborate ones track appreciation in value, offer background information about vineyards and vintners, and even include comments from famous wine tasters. Anyone who collects wines as a hobby and has the time to click from one window to another to call up suppliers, purchase prices, predicted maturing dates, and taste impressions is bound to find managing his cellar on computer a pleasant occupation. And anyone who buys wine as an investment absolutely requires the appropriate software. Each program, to be sure, is set up differently. Some cover only top international wines and provide all the information that is of importance to the investor, from details about the wine's production to the latest auction prices. Others are more general, offering useful information about wine and specific help for the amateur, such as general facts about the growing region, or listings of largely unknown wines.

Further Information

Currently the most sophisticated (and expensive) program for cellar management is *Robert Parker's Wine Advisor and Cellar Manager.* Highly visual in organization, it offers a detailed overview of your own cellar as well as useful information about 28,000 wines. By means of a link to the database at Parker's newsletter the *Wine Advocate,* the user also has access to all 34,000 of this publication's evaluations and descriptions by the "wine pope." A practical alternative for the more casual wine drinker, the *American Wine Cellar* program was developed for home use (www.vca-shop.de or www.homebox.de). In addition to cellar management, it contains suggestions about which wines go well with specific standard dishes.

Practical: The *American Wine Cellar* program was developed for home use. In addition to cellar management, it contains suggestions about which wine goes well with which food or dish (www.vca-shop.de or www.homebox.de).

WINES FROM BIRTH YEARS

Today many people lay in wines from the years in which their children were born. This lovely gesture has only one drawback: not every year produces wines of a quality to stand up to twenty years or more of aging. What to do if the year was a minor vintage? Simple: first check to see which growing regions produce long-lived wines and how their vintages have performed. Then decide whether to buy normal bottles or large-format ones, which age better and more slowly than those in small bottles as well as holding their value better. And when should you buy? Purchase white wines a year after the harvest, likewise Bordeaux, when it is sold by subscription. Red wines of other regions are not released until from two to four years after the harvest.

Buying Wine

New vinothèques and oenotèques are springing up all over. Restaurants are offering their wines at cash-and-carry prices. On the Internet, e-commerce in wine is booming. Mail-order houses are offering wines by catalog, and vintners are offering free shipping. Buying wine has become easier—but by no means simpler.

More Show than Substance

There are wines whose best feature is their packaging. Label and packaging designers have done their best to give the wine an impressive look, though the contents of the bottle can be sadly mediocre—or worse. With the revival of wine drinking, consumers are confronted with a flood of ordinary wines distinguished mainly by colorful labels, evocative names, breathtaking bottle shapes, and none-too-low prices. An enraged wine critic has described the taste of most proseccos currently on the market for less than 5 Euros (about $6) as "shaving lotion with carbon dioxide." Vintner's prospectuses rave about "lifestyle" and "*savoir vivre*." Potential buyers whose judgment is not yet assured can easily be misled. They need comparisons and good advice, but instead they are offered "worlds of wine experience" and "easy purchase."

Grocery Stores

Grocery stores often have a small wine assortment. Choice is limited, as a rule, and quality not very high. Frequently knowledgeable advice is unavailable. The exceptions are fine delicatessens and department stores with large grocery departments, which not infrequently have a well-selected wine display stocked with both simple, everyday wines and expensive

vintages. These stores are very committed to providing advice, and some are fully as competent as the best wine shops.

Supermarkets

These establishments specialize in cheap wines and are mainly concerned with turnover. The majority of the industrial wines bought up from all over the world await undemanding buyers on their shelves. Favorite offerings are overstocks, undated wines, and wines with no clear designation of origin.

Mail-Order Buying

Large mail-order houses have recently added wines to their offerings. Since their understanding of wines is limited, they concentrate on commercial brands or wines from well-known producers. Here you will frequently find bottles with designer labels and wines in gift packaging for people more concerned with appearance than quality.

A cheap wine with a well-known name in elaborate packaging.

Discounters

Consumer warehouses that also cater to retailers have captured an increasing share in the wine market, often selling wines only by the carton. It can be difficult for the inexperienced shopper to find his way around: cheap wines from all over the world stand next to top-quality vintages, dealers' wines next to estate-bottled vintages. You will find a large number of low-quality wines from well-known growing regions whose names suggest quality (Bordeaux, for example), plagiarized labels or names that the naive buyer can easily confuse with a superior original, and wines from unknown bottlers whose imposing names suggest to the layman quality and exclusiveness. Of the top wines, generally only mediocre or poor vintages are represented, which the nonprofessional cannot be expected to recognize.

Professional Wine Dealers

Professional wine dealers are the backbone of the wine business. As a rule they maintain retail shops in which the customer—whether a wine layman or a more experienced buyer—is provided with competent and pertinent advice. Many of them offer open wines for tasting, sponsor informative wine samplings or seminars, and offer individualized service. They enjoy the trust of buyers and know their preferences, so that they can make specific recommendations to them. Some have multiple branches, affiliated agencies, or franchise dealers. Certain dealers specialize in the wines of a specific country, while others carry an international assortment. For many, that wine is not only a livelihood but also a passion is perfectly evident in the depth of their knowledge. They are familiar with growing regions, maintain contact with vintners, have tasting experience, study the trade journals, and attend professional seminars and fairs. The buyer is given sound advice, and even provided with insider information if he wishes it.

Mail-Order Wine Merchants

Some professional wine dealers have given up their shops and turned to mail order, selling by catalog. Many top-quality wines, especially, are now ordered and shipped by this route. By studying the catalog, you soon discover whether you are dealing with true experts or people only pretending to know what they are selling. Competent wine dealers import at least some of their wines themselves and represent not only the large, well-known estates but also smaller, unknown ones. Under certain conditions, since the customer has no chance to taste the wine before buying, they will offer a presorted trial package.

Wine Auctions

Compared to the total size of the wine market, the quantity bought and sold at auction is minimal. But in the high-end wine market auctions play a major role, especially for lovers of older vintages and wine in larger bottles. In the last few years, the number of more recent vintages sold at auction has also increased. But it is worth noting that the hammer prices for many wines are higher than those charged by professional wine dealers, once you figure in taxes, handling charges, and transportation. Great buys are rare. In Internet auctions, especially, people frequently pay prices that are far too high. Only a few auction houses reliably inspect the wares they accept. For wines that are more than twenty years old, an indication of the fill level is of great importance. If the information is incorrect, it is the buyer who loses.

Internet Wine Trading

Buying wine on the Internet is the newest trend. The number of Internet wine dealers is constantly growing; the lion's share of the market, however, is still shared by a small number of e-commerce concerns, most of them offshoots of large wine importers or shipping companies that already have the necessary policies and infrastructures. Wines purchased in this way are mainly of very basic quality. Rarities of the quality that connoisseurs look for are hard to find on the Internet, and if available at all, they are offered by smaller specialists. Web sites, designed to be customer-friendly, frequently include more than simple lists of wines for sale. Brightened up with colorful pictures of wine bottles and labels, they also offer wine accessories like carafes, glasses, and corkscrews. Listings come with detailed descriptions of the wine region and production method, quality and aging potential, and tips on matching wines with specific dishes. Skeptics can order trial packets, take part in virtual wine tastings, or request specific advice. The customer's enthusiasm for e-commerce, however, is frequently squelched on receipt of the goods. Aside from broken bottles, shipping delays, and higher-than-expected transport costs or duties, the listings may be out of date and the wines requested no longer available. Experienced Internet shoppers ask about terms: free shipping on orders above a certain value, the right to return wines they are not satisfied with, and payment only on receipt of the shipment should be guaranteed.

Wine as a Capital Investment

Bankers can differentiate between savings-account interest and investment yield. Wine collectors, however, have a hard time distinguishing between drinking wines and investment wines. Many are convinced that they have good investments in their cellars, firmly believing that everything that cost a lot of money is going to make them a lot of money if they someday put it up for sale at a wine auction. An expensive error.

Wine Auctions

There have been wine auctions ever since wines began being bottled and corked. The London auction house Christie's auctioned its first lot of fine Bordeaux and Madeira wines in 1766. Until only a few years ago, many wine auctions were events at which only aged wines were bought and sold. The wines of the great 1847 vintage in Bordeaux were the first to be treated as investments. When the British government lowered tariffs on French wines, prices shot up to unheard-of levels. A second great wave of speculation began in 1959, when the French franc was devalued, and for the first time dealers from the United State bought up Bordeaux wines in massive quantities. Only in 1972, after that year's vintage

had been sold for overly high prices, did the Bordeaux wine market collapse. But things calmed down again in a few years. Then came the miraculous vintage of 1982, which once again heated up the speculation that has continued to this day.

The Yield

The profits to be made through investment in wine can vary from zero to 100 percent per year. They are now made not with aged wines but with young ones. To land a 100-percent hit, you need luck, good connections in the wine business, and the information letter *The Wine Advocate,* published by the American wine tester Robert Parker. A wine that he rates with 99 or 100 points is bound to double in price in a matter of weeks. If you don't already have it in your cellar (or have futures on it), you'll need good contacts with dealers or brokers to still buy a few

Auctions are an important venue for trading top wines.

bottles at a favorable price. To get a bottle of the famous Château Pétrus, money alone will not suffice. The few bottles available are offered to good, long-term customers. Or it may be coupled: if you buy other, less rare wines for a generous price, some dealers will throw in a bottle of Pétrus.

In addition to old wines, today's auction market increasingly deals in young ones.

Cult Wines

Professional wine speculation is limited to a few cult red wines. Most are *premiers grands crus* or *deuxièmes grands crus* from Bordeaux. Only a few wines from other growing regions and countries are equally suited for speculation and the investment of capital. In addition, there are, worldwide, a few dozen connoisseurs' wines available in only tiny quantities and with very limited market. The risk is high, however. Common to all these wines is that they are not available in unlimited quantities. Bordeaux wines are usually sold while they are still aging in the barrel. As a rule, that is when they are cheapest. The right to receive a case of a specific wine once it had been released is called a "future." When the wine is finally released (after two and a half years), the future may have already changed hands any number of times—each time with a profit if all goes well. Wine auctions are not needed at all; brokers take care of the business.

Speculation in Vintages

Frequently only specific years capture the interest of speculators. In the ten years following 1985, when they were released, the *premiers grands crus* of the famous 1982 Bordeaux vintage rose in price by 700 to 1,000 percent. That represents up to a 100-percent increase in value a year. The 1983 vintage, by contrast, yielded only 15 percent. Moreover, it can happen that a 100-point Parker wine is subsequently downgraded and immediately loses value, though of course a wine can be upgraded as well. You also have to figure in changes in exchange rates and auction fees. The large auction houses take a premium of between 10 and 15 percent of the knock-down price from both the buyer and the seller. Then come packing fees, lot fees, shipping fees, and insurance costs—all of which reduce your profit.

THE 30 BLUE-CHIP WINES

- Château Mouton-Rothschild/ Bordeaux
- Château Lafite-Rothschild/ Bordeaux
- Château Latour/Bordeaux
- Château Léoville Las Cases/ Bordeaux
- Château Picon Lalande/Bordeaux
- Château Margaux/Bordeaux
- Château Haut-Brion/Bordeaux
- Château d'Yquem/Bordeaux
- Château Ausone/Bordeaux
- Château Cheval Blanc/Bordeaux
- La Mondotte/Bordeaux
- Valandraut/Bordeaux
- Château Pétrus/Bordeaux
- Le Pin/Bordeaux
- Château l'Eglise Clinet/Bordeaux
- Château Lafleur/Bordeaux
- Domaine Romanée Conti/ Burgundy
- Hermitage La Chapelle/Rhône
- Vega Sicilia/Spain
- Pingus/Spain
- L'Ermità/Spain
- Sassicaia/Italy
- Ornellaia/Italy
- Grange/Australia
- Hill of Grace/Australia
- Opus One/California
- Dominus/California
- Harlan Estate/California
- Screaming Eagle/California
- Bryant Family/California

TIPS & TRICKS: FACTORS THAT INCREASE VALUE

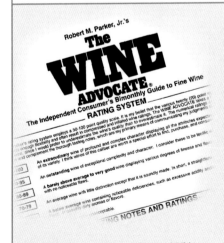

The Wine Advocate, the undisputed Bible for wine investors around the world.

It adds to the value if wines are offered in their original cases or cartons. Especially sought after are larger bottles containing from 1.5 to a maximum of 12 liters. These are rare, and wine ages better in them. In old wines, people look for undamaged capsules as well as undamaged labels. This is especially true of wines from Château Mouton Rothschild, which are collected for their artists' labels. Extremely important is the fill level of the bottle. The higher the level the less risk that the quality has been compromised.

The wines from Bordeaux's Château Latour keep their value as well as any wines in the world.

Wine and Food

Over the centuries, wine in Mediterranean countries has been a
staple, not just a drink for holidays. It has been used in daily
cooking and drunk at everyday meals. Classic combinations
of local wines and regional cuisines have evolved. Today
there is much debate about which wine goes with what
dish and why, and at least one insight has come out
of it: Wine drinkers and cooks are more inventive
than purists tend to think.

Tagliatelle al Lepre

This dish is listed among the specials in every Tuscan trattoria. The sauce of stewed hare cooks on the fire for around six hours, with the constant addition of wine, which can be a Brunello di Montalcino or a Chianti, a Vino Nobile or Carmignano. The only requirement is that the wine have the aroma of game, berries, and spices typical of wines from Tuscany.

Leg of Lamb with Bordeaux: A classic. With lamb you can also choose a Bandol, a Châteauneuf-du-Pape, a Rioga, a Ribera del Duero, or a Shiraz.

Spaghetti Vongole: A Sardinian Vermentino or a Verdicchio from the Marches goes wonderfully well with this typical Mediterranean dish; a good Provençal rosé is perfect.

Brioche: French cooks appear to have invented this yeast bread made of eggs, butter, and flour for the sole purpose of enhancing the taste of Champagne.

San Daniele Ham and Prosecco: A superb duo—but Cava and Spanish Serrano ham are an equally good pair.

TIPS & TRICKS: GRAPPA AND CIGARETTES

Smokers can also enjoy wine, but nicotine and wine don't go together. Nicotine stimulates the taste buds so strongly that they are deadened at least 15 minutes after the last drag from a cigarette. Much the same is true of espresso or coffee. It is as difficult to taste the subtleties of a wine after drinking caffeine as it is after a highly spiced Mexican meal. The only wines that do not fall flat on the palate after coffee, cigarettes, cigars, or other tobaccos are fortified sweet wines: Port, Madeira, Marsala, or an oloroso Sherry. They refresh the tongue. Wood-aged grappa, Calvados, and Cognac combine perfectly with a smoke.

Sole à la Dieppe

In northern France and Belgium, Dieppe sole is a culinary milestone: A fresh-caught fish is prepared with whipped crab butter with mussels or shrimp and served with a buttery-soft, mineral-rich Meursault. Of course, other combinations are possible, but this one approaches perfection.

Shrimp with Glass Noodles: With seafood prepared with Asian spices, a semi-dry German Riesling or an Australian Chardonnay are ideal.

Lobster: Crustaceans adorn menus all over the world. Almost always they are served with Chardonnay. Also good are a hearty Chenin Blanc or a Viognier.

Goat Cheese: This cheese is produced in many countries, but only the cheese-loving country of France has discovered the ideal complement: a Sancerre.

Grilled Steak

A love of red meat is apparent not only in steak houses but also in fine restaurants. A sirloin or porterhouse steak grilled over wood is a delight— a classic dish for a young, tannin-rich Cabernet Sauvignon, perhaps from California. The juice of the rare meat and the tannin go together, as well as the grilled taste and the toast aromas that come from aging in wood barrels.

Coq-au-Vin and Burgundy: A dish that con-
quered the world—in Burgundy it is part of every
cook's repertoire. The same wine used for simmering the chicken is served at the table.

Venison Fillet: A fruity, sweet Pinot Noir, a
German Spätburgunder, a Swiss Blaubur-
gunder, or a Syrah from the Rhône go well
with its sourish, astringent taste.

Foie Gras: It would be only half so famous
if the French didn't have the nobly sweet
Sauternes to go with it. They are as though
made for each other. Other nobly sweet
wines are also suitable.

And Finally: The Ten Most

Wine inspires people's imaginations. It often happens that the boundary between truth and imagination eventually blurs. In any

1 The Best Wines Come from France

France's reputation as the superior wine nation rests on its great wines from Burgundy and Bordeaux. They represent roughly five percent of the country's wine production. The other wines from France are just as good or just as mediocre as those of other wine nations. Moreover, not all Bordeaux and Burgundy wines are great. Only a very small number can claim to be extraordinary. And top-quality wines are produced in Spain, Italy, California, Australia, Austria, and Germany as well. Some of them have received higher ratings in blind tastings than their French counterparts—even from French wine tasters.

Not all French wines are from Bordeaux.

2 There Are No Longer Any Good Wines for Under $15

It is true that wine prices have exploded in the past few years. But at the same time, the quality of many wines has risen dramatically. For those looking for good wines for less that $15 there are a number of wine guides dedicated to just that. And there are wine journals that regularly present good wines for under $10. But this does not mean that all those costing $10 are worth the money.

3 Only Good Vintages Are Worth Buying

Cool or damp years no longer have the same dire effects on wine quality that they once did. Staggered harvests, rapid transport, and better sorting of grapes ensure that even wines from "lesser" vintages are true to type. Their only disadvantages compared to "great" vintages is that they lack fullness and should be consumed sooner.

4 Old Wines Are Good Wines

The myth tells us that wines are meant to age. Yet many people make a face when they open an old bottle and try the wine: strange smells, stale aromas, bizarre taste nuances. Suddenly they feel a craving for a fresh, young wine—often with justification. By no means does every wine improve with age; many that are left undisturbed for ten or twenty years should really have been drunk after five. What is important to remember is that every wine reaches a peak, and for many, this is in the first or second year.

5 Women Prefer Pink Champagne

Salmon-colored rosé Champagne is reputed to be the favorite drink of women on festive occasions. A genuine compliment, for because of its higher Pinot Noir content, rosé is one of the most elegant of all Champagnes. But all consumer studies show that women drink considerable more "white" Champagne than rosé. So is this only an advertising gimmick? Or perhaps the perpetuation of the fantasy of men who once associated the delicate pink of the wine with the "gentle sex"? Or is it simply because rosé Champagnes generally receive a higher dose of sugar and therefore taste slightly sweeter than brut Champagnes? This would imply another myth, namely that women prefer sweet wines. The truth is that it is mainly men who buy Champagne. And as for rosé Champagne, there is no reason to believe that men would buy it if they didn't like it themselves.

Rosé Champagne: a delicately pink sparkling wine.

Persistent Myths about Wine

case, there are only a few aspects of life in which people so shamelessly defend their mistaken ideas as they do about wine.

6 Heavy Red Wines Ought to Be Drunk by the Fireplace

If this were true, red wine consumption would be dramatically lower than it is. How many people own a fireplace anymore? This prejudice comes from a time when fireplaces and fiery red wines were the only sources of heat in a house. Since the arrival of central heating, things have changed. Heavy red wines taste just as wonderful at the dining table or the kitchen counter.

7 Only Dry Wines Are Good Wines

What does dry mean? Zero ounces (o grams) of residual sugar, that is to say completely fermented? Such wines are rare. A maximum of 1 oz. (4 grams) of residual sugar? That is the rule in the European Union. A maximum of 3 oz. (9 grams) of residual sugar? According to German wine law even these wines can still be considered dry. Or 5 oz. (15 grams) of residual sugar, as brut Champagnes are allowed? The confusing thing is that many bruts and many German 9-gram-residual-sugar wines taste dryer than other wines with only one-fifteenth an ounce (4 grams) of residual sugar. A high alcohol-content gives the wine a fruitiness, even though analysis declares it to be dry. High acid, on the other hand, balances out the available sweetness. So the question remains whether a noticeably sweet wine is unpleasant to drink. That, in turn, depends on a person's individual taste. The fact is that some of the best Alsatian, German, and Austrian Rieslings reveal a noticeable

residual sweetness and are nevertheless extremely elegant, to say nothing of the countless botrytized wines that are among the most expensive and sought-after wines in the world. In contrast to white Zinfandel, which Americans are fond of, Riesling is a lemonade-like, technically sweet white wine.

8 Women Make the Best Wine Tasters

A controversial assertion that is confirmed just as often as it is disproved. It is possible that women often perceive a wine's aromas more spontaneously and are more imaginative in naming them. But that proves only that proficient women are just as successful in the wine business as proficient men.

9 People Prefer Drinking White and Rosé Wines in Summer

Many prejudices are persistent because they are related to pleasant associations. Terraces in Tuscany, for example, or expansive beaches dotted in summer with people relaxing with a glass of chilled wine. As though it were never cold in summer, or rainy. As though in summer people never hanker for a steak or pork roast. As though a well-tempered red wine did not taste exquisite on a terrace by the sea in summer—as wonderful as a noble white wine in winter.

10 Non-European Wines Cannot Age

It may be that red wines from California, Chile, Australia, and South Africa do not have the legendary potential for aging that some of Europe's top-quality wines have. But in countless wine tastings, it has been discovered that twenty years old is no great age for the best non-European vintages. Moreover, there is much to suggest that great Bordeaux wines will not be so long-lived as those from fifty years ago owing to changes in production methods. The châteaus are now more concerned with assuring their wines of a high degree of maturity and finesse at an earlier age.

Wines from the New World. The best may not age for one hundred years but are certainly capable of aging for twenty.

AOC: French, *appellation contrôlée,* designation of origin, the shortened form of *appellation d'origine contrôlée* (AOC)

Air Tone: slightly oxidized wine

Aroma: a wine taste that is perceived by the nose

Assemblage: the blending of identical wines or wines of identical origin

Barrique: a small (225 l) oak barrel

Bocksbeutel: a flat-bellied wine bottle

Body: the total of a wine's alcohol and extract

Botrytis: noble rot; a desirable appearance of mold, especially on grapes meant for sweet wines

Bouquet: the totality of a wine's aroma impressions

Brut: literally, dry; in fact, up to 15 grams of sugar are permitted

Cava: Spanish sparkling wine made by the *méthode champenoise*

Château: castle, wine estate

Chewing: making chewing motions while tasting ensures that the wine comes into contact with all the tongue's taste buds

Claret: English term for red Bordeaux wine

Clos: French, a closed-off vineyard, often surrounded by a wall

Crémant: sparkling wine with only slight effervescence

Cru: French, single vineyard

Cuvée: French, 1. a blend of identical wines or wines of the same origin; 2. during winemaking, the first runoff and most valuable part of the must

Decanting: pouring wine from the bottle into a carafe

Degorging: removing the provisional cork from the Champagne bottle after bottle fermentation for the purpose of removing the yeast, generally accomplished in an ice bath

Degustation: professional wine testing; the wine is not swallowed but generally spit out after tasting

Dépôt: sediment of a red wine formed in the bottle, a sign of high quality

Designation of origin: the name of a quality winegrowing region, also called "origin designation"

Diabetic Wine: wine with no more than 4 grams of residual sugar

DO: Spanish, *denominación de origen,* an official designation of origin

DOC: Italian, *denominazione de origine controllata,* an official designation of origin

DOCG: Italian, *denominazione de origine controllata e garantita,* official and guaranteed designation of origin, the highest level of Italy's designations of quality

Domaine: French, country vineyard

Dosage: mixture of wine and sugar (occasionally brandy and sugar) often added to sparkling wines to round out the taste

Dry: term for a wine in which you taste no residual sweetness. According to EU standards, the formula for "dry" reads: acid in milligrams minus 2. In practice, wines containing up to a maximum of 4 grams of residual sugar are labeled "dry"

Extract: the substances that remain in the wine after the evaporation of the water, for example higher-quality alcohols, acids, minerals, sugar

Fiery: designation for a heavy, alcohol-rich wine

Finesse: French expression for a wine's elegance

Fining: the stabilization of the wine with bentonite, egg white, isinglass, etc., to prevent it from clouding in the bottle

Finish: the taste of a wine that lingers in the mouth after it is swallowed; the longer the better

Fortified: a wine to which pure, high-percentage alcohol has been added; the yeast is killed off, and the residual sugar cannot react further. German wines may not be laced

Frizzante: slightly sparkling wine, often thanks to added carbon dioxide

Gesprizter: Austrian, a light wine thinned with water

Heuriger: Austrian, 1. a young wine, 2. a wine tavern

Ice Wine: wine made from grapes that are frozen and harvested late. In Germany it must have at least the must weight of a beerenauslese

Lactic Acid: a mild acid formed by bacteria whose final product is hard malic acid

Light: slight in body, especially in alcohol content

Magnum: a large bottle containing 1.5 L, or twice that of a standard bottle

Malolactic fermentation: fermentation of lactic acid, the transformation of malic acid into lactic acid

Maturation: French *élévage,* the improvement of newly fermented wines in wooden barrels or steel tanks

Mild: in Germany, the customary designation for wines with more than 18 grams of residual sugar, which because of the strong acid taste delicately sweet, but not cloying

Millésime: French, vintage

Mousse: the foam of Champagne and Sekt

Noble rot: see Botrytis

Nose: term for a wine's bouquet

Öchsle: unit of measure for the physical density of the must, from which conclusions can be made about its sugar content

Oxidized: negative characteristic of a wine that has become unpalatable because of age or excessive contact with air; in Sherry, Port, and other fortified wines, a necessary feature of maturity

Perlage: the effervescence of sparkling wines in the glass

Pomace: the grape skins after pressing

Prädikat: description of a quality wine in Germany and sometimes in Austria depending on the sugar content of its must: Kabinett, Spätlese, Auslese, etc.

QbA: German, *Qualitätswein bestimmter Anbaugebiete,* quality wine from a specific growing region; in Germany, the lowest level of quality wine

Producer bottled: wine that is bottled by the same vineyard that produced the grapes

Racking: siphoning off the red wine from the skins, the white wine from the yeast

Reductive: fermented, matured, and bottled with minimal contact with oxygen; the opposite of oxidative

Reserva: Spanish, wine with an extended aging period, measured differently from one growing region to another

Riserva: Italian, a wine aged for a long time, often the same as an auslese

Seasoning: pouring a small amount of a new wine into the glass, swirling it around, then pouring it out so as to remove the aromas of the previous wine

Secondary Fermentation: 1. Further fermentation of red wine in the tank after racking, 2. Unwanted further fermentation of the wine in the bottle

Semi-Dry: in Germany up to 18 grams residual sugar, in Champagne ("extra-sec") up to 20 grams

Smaragd: the highest designation of wines from the Wachau, roughly equivalent to a German Spätlese

Sommelier: French designation for a wine steward

Sparkling Wine: the collective term for Champagne, Sekt, Spumante, and other effervescent wines

Spritzig: wine with a residue of carbon dioxide, frequently young wines

Spumante: Italian, sparkling wine

Steinfeder: a level in the designation of wines form the Wachau, roughly equivalent to a German QbA

Süssreserve: sulfured and sweetened must added to the wine after it has been thoroughly fermented, permitted in Germany for sweetening

Table wines: the lowest category of wines in European wine law, with modest requirements with regard to quality

Tannic acid: tannin; an acid present especially in red wines, bitter to the taste and sharp on the tongue, that becomes more mellow over the years, preserving the wine and lending it fullness and complexity

Tannin: another term for tannic acid, one of the group of polyphenoles and found primarily in red wines

Tartar: the precipitate of tartaric acid, can appear even during fermentation, but also later in the form of small white crystals in the bottom of the bottle; in no way affects the taste

Ullage: the space between the cork and the wine in a wine bottle

Vinification: the wine-making process, pressing and fermentation of the must

VQPRD: French, *Vins de Qualité Produits dans des Régions Déterminées.* In European wine law, all quality wines from specific growing regions receive this designation

Accessories

Apex Wine Cellars
13219 Northup Way, suite 200
Bellevue, WA 98005
Telephone: (425) 644-1178;
(800) 462-2714
Fax: (425) 644-1049
Web site: www.apexwinecellars.com

Artisans on Web
552 Broadway, 4R
New York, NY 10012
Telephone: (866) 237-0602
Fax: (917) 237-0601
Web site: www.aoweb.com

Baron
1164 Thomas Street
Seattle, WA 98109
Telephone: (800) 938-5008
Web site: www.baronweb.com

Corkscrew Mart
2880 Zanker Road, suite 203
San Jose, CA 95134
Telephone: (408) 892-8900
Web site: www.corkscrew-mart.com

Evineyard.com
1200 NW Naito Parkway, suite 220
Portland, OR 97209
Telephone: (877) 289-6886
Web site: www.evineyard.com

Imagery Products
P.O. Box 13810
San Luis Obispo, CA 93406
Telephone: (888) 459-9463
Fax: (805) 783-2040
Web site: www.imageryproducts.com

International Wine Accessories
10246 Miller Road
Dallas, TX 75238-1206
Telephone: 1 (214) 349-6097;
(800) 527-4072
Fax: 1 (214) 349-8712
Web site: iwawine.com

Screwpull/Le Creuset
P.O. Box 67
Early Branch, SC 29916
Telephone: (803) 943-4308;
(877) Creuset
Fax: (803) 943-4510
Web site: www.lecreuset.com

Wineaccents.com
858 West Armitage, suite 115
Chicago, IL 60614
Telephone: (773) 665-9375
Web site: www.wineaccents.com

Wine Appreciation Guild
360 Swift Avenue, unit 34
South San Francisco, CA 94080
Telephone: (650) 866-3020
Fax: (650) 866-3513
Web site: www.wineappreciation.com

Wine.com
570 Gateway Drive
Napa, CA 94558
Telephone: (707) 299-3200;
(888) 946-3789
Fax: (707) 265-9165
Web site: www.wine.com

The Wine Enthusiast
P.O. Box 39
Pleasantville, NY 10570-0039
Telephone: (800) 356-8466
Fax: (800) 833-8466
Web site: www.wineenthusiast.com

Stemware

Marjorie Lumm's Wine Glasses
112 Pine Street
San Anselmo, CA 94960
Telephone: (415) 454-0660;
(800) 806-0677
Fax: (415) 454-4486
Web site: www.wineglassesltd.com

Riedel
A-6330 Kufstein
Austria
Telephone: 43 5372 64896
Fax: 43 5372 63225
Web site: www.riedelcrystal.com

Spiegelau
Hauptstrasse 2-4
D-94518 Spiegelau
Web site: www.spiegelau.com

Wine Stuff
81 Carleton Avenue
Central Islip, NY 11722
Telephone: (800) Winestuff
Web site: www.wineglasses.com;
www.decanters.com

Software

WineBase
Almost Vertical Software
P.O. Box 221
Black Rock VIC 3193
Australia
Telephone: 61 3 9580 2100
Fax: 61 3 9580 0655
Web site: www.winebase.com.au

Wine Technologies
P.O. Box 67465
Chestnut Hill, MA 02467
Telephone: (617) 323-8745
Fax: (617) 323-3878
Web site: www.winetech.com

General

The Conran Shop
U.S.: 407 East 59th Street
New York, NY 10022
Telephone: (212) 755-9079
U.K.: Michelin House, 81 Fulham Road
London, SW3 6RD
Telephone: (020) 7589 7401
Web site: www.conran.co.uk

Crate and Barrel
Telephone: (800) 967-6696

Dean and Deluca
Telephone: (877) 826-9246 or
(316) 838-1255

Kitchen Etc.
Web site: www.kitchenetc.com

Lechters
Web site: www.lechtersonline.com

Pottery Barn
Telephone: (800) 922-5507
Web site: www.potterybarn.com

Sur La Table
Telephone: (800) 243-0852
Web site: www.surlatable.com

Williams-Sonoma Inc.
1175 Madison Avenue
New York, NY 10028
Telephone: (212) 289-6832
Web site: www.williamssonomainc.com

PHOTO CREDITS